# How to Take Notes, Read Better, and Retain It All:

*Master Your Information, Master Your Learning and Performance*

By Peter Hollins,

Author and Researcher at

petehollins.com

## Table of Contents

### Chapter One: Note Taking Nuts and Bolts __ 6

- The Sentence Method _____ 10
- The Charting Method _____ 17
- Get the GIST _____ 26
- Chunking Information _____ 33

### Chapter Two: Thinking in Hierarchies to Get Organized _____ 45

- Mind Mapping _____ 45
- The QEC Method _____ 53
- The 80/20 Rule or Pareto Principle _____ 61
- Knowledge Organization with Zettelkasten 68

### Chapter Three: Strengthen Your Reading Comprehension _____ 79

- Effective Highlighting _____ 80
- Active Listening and Note Taking _____ 86
- Top-down Self-questioning for Deeper Comprehension _____ 93
- Reverse outlining for better reading comprehension _____ 99

### Chapter Four: Deeper Comprehension and Lasting Memory _____ 109

Writing by Hand Increases Memory _____ 110

Schema Activation in Reading Comprehension _____ 116

The Art of Observational Note Taking _____ 122

Overlearning for Subject Mastery _____ 133

## Chapter Five: Master Abstraction, Analysis, and Critical Thinking _____ 143

Reading Analytically Through Pigeonholing _____ 144

The Three Level Reading Guide–from Shallow to Deep _____ 152

The SPE Method for Better Critical Reading _____ 158

ADEPT Method _____ 165

## Chapter Six: Analyze and Synthesize ____ 175

Compile a KWL Chart _____ 176

The REST Method _____ 181

How to Filter What You Consume _____ 186

Becoming a Syntopical Reader _____ 192

Chapter One: Note Taking Nuts and Bolts

What do think of when you hear the phrase, "note taking"?

You might assume that note taking is a basic skill that simply exists to help people record information. Perhaps you see it as a practical way to aid your memory, taking quick notes so you don't forget this or that. In the chapters that follow, however, I hope to convince you that the art of note taking is much, much more than this.

While this book is about note taking, it's also about the magic that happens inside our own brains when we learn, challenge, and interpret information. **Well written notes will help you explore and reflect on the complexities of your learning processes, making them**

**essential for clear, powerful, and organized thinking.**

Taking high-quality notes is a valuable life skill that's well worth cultivating. There is plenty of advice out there about various note taking strategies, but our aim is not to just collect a series of tips and tools, but rather to develop our own intellectual powers, so that we are always empowered to use just the right tool, and in just the right way.

Whether you're a school or university student, someone who wants to improve their writing and reading comprehension, or simply studying for your own edification and development, **note taking is a skill that will teach you to learn**, and there is no subject in the world it cannot be applied to.

As with anything in life, you get out what you put in. Many of the approaches and techniques covered in this book may appear at first glance to be simple and straightforward, but their power comes in their *application*. Good note taking is active, responsive, and tailored to our unique goals and needs. It requires patience, consistency, and discretion. The same principle applies to reading this book–the way to make these concepts come alive is to test them out yourself, tailor them, and make them your own.

With each chapter, the techniques and methods we explore will increase in complexity, but with active engagement, so too will your own comprehension and mastery.

Let's start at the beginning: When you take notes, what are you *actually* doing? In the most practical sense, how are you using your pen and paper, and precisely what are you writing down?

Most of us have ended up with our own style and approach for taking notes without giving it much thought; we simply turn up to a text or a lecture and start making marks on a page. In this chapter, however, we'll be looking at some more deliberate forms of note taking. This is not an exhaustive list, but a collection of the most effective practical techniques, and the rationale behind them. We'll consider their respective pros and cons and their applicability to different areas of study.

## The Sentence Method

**The sentence method** described below **helps you clearly separate out–literally–the new ideas, thoughts, and themes you're taking in.** This method is easy, but takes a little practice. It requires us to be slower and more deliberate in the way we listen, and to resist the tendency to race ahead in our own minds.

The idea is to organize and understand *while* you process new information, and to do so using complete sentences, each spaced on a new line on the page. While best suited to live lectures, this method can also be used to quickly make sense of new readings or to create quick summaries that can then be used later to draft essays of your own.

At first, this method may seem a little tedious or time-consuming, but being deliberate in this way is precisely what makes it so effective. As you carefully prepare incoming data in sentence form, you are also shaping and organizing those ideas into a logical, organized structure.

The method is straightforward:

1. Identify the broad topic and the main points you'll be covering
2. Add details to each of these main points, in the form of full sentences
3. As you add these details, give each sentence a new line

That's it. It may sound simple, but you'd be surprised just how often your notes *don't* conform to so simple a criterion. Let's take a closer look using examples to illustrate the process. One example will be fairly basic and the other more complex, to show that although simple, the method works for topics of any kind.

## Step 1: Identify broad topic and main points

Let's say you're listening to a quick video lecture about the key differences and similarities between viral and bacterial infections. The broad topic is obviously types of infection, and there are two main points to be covered–the characteristics of both bacteria and viruses, and how they compare.

At the top of your page, you would write the topic header "types of infection: viral vs bacterial". Then, beneath that, list out the main points: "Differences" and "similarities". This gives you a strong outline for the notes you take throughout the lecture.

You might, on the other hand, have a live lecture about the many consequences of the Reformation on society. "The effects of the reformation" is clearly the broad topic, but this topic will likely have many different points and sub-points, many of which you don't yet know about.

In this example, you'd place the header, "effects of the Reformation" at the top of your page. Then, as the lecture continues you would listen for important main points to add, such as "social changes," "economic changes," or "religious changes" when they come up.

**Step 2: Add details in the form of full sentences**

Now you can expand on each point with concise sentences that cover just one idea each. A good sentence will be clearly connected to the broader topic and will usually state a fact or piece of data, explain a process, summarize, or connect certain ideas.

For our virus and bacteria example, under the main point "differences" you might list the following sentences:

- Bacteria can live and replicate on its own, but viruses need a host to replicate.
- Some bacteria are helpful to humans, whereas there are no beneficial viruses.
- Viruses are not technically alive, but bacteria are living cellular organisms.

For the Reformation example, you might write:

- The Protestant emphasis on personal Bible reading led to dramatic increases in literacy. (This could be placed beneath the sub-point of "social changes".)
- The closure of monasteries and restructuring of churches resulted in significant wealth transfer away from the church and to the nobility. (This could fit beneath "economic changes".)
- Challenges to Papal authority had far-reaching consequences for the political and spiritual organization of the church. (This would fit beneath "religious changes".)

## Step 3: Give each new sentence its own line

As you might have guessed, you will probably be adding sub-sentences and sub-sub-sentences to your growing outline as you listen to the lecture or make your way through the text. This is why it's important to give yourself plenty of space so that you can expand on your notes as needed. Not only will this give you a little visual clarity, it will also help you understand these ideas relative to one another.

As the lecture on the Reformation unfolds, for example, you might find yourself with this sort of structure:

- Social changes as a result of the Reformation:
    - The Reformation led to social changes that ultimately laid the foundation for modern democracy.
        - One social change was the increasing value placed on education.

- Another social change was the increasing value placed on personal conscience.

As you can see, the larger and more complex your topic, the greater the likelihood that you will have more nested layers like above. Plan ahead by giving yourself enough space.

Pros and Cons

*The sentence method has many attractive features:*

- **It's precise.** Full, grammatically correct sentences encourage you to clearly capture ideas and concepts in neat, concise chunks. This may at first seem simple, but it's an underdeveloped skill, and most of us tend to take fractured, disconnected notes that lack this clarity. Taking clear notes trains you to think clear thoughts, while simultaneously producing a useful written record that is neat, logical, and structured.
- **It's adaptable.** You can use this method for *any* topic, including information that is either more quantitative (facts, details) or qualitative (themes, narratives).

- **It's thorough.** Done correctly, the notes you produce will paint a comprehensive picture of the topic.

*There are some drawbacks to be mindful of, however:*

- **It's cumbersome.** Depending on your topic, you may end up creating enormous and ungainly amounts of written text.. When you're overwhelmed by information, important points can easily be lost.
- **It's slow.** This method may be less appropriate for live lectures if your writing or typing speed cannot keep up with the pace of the lecture. It can also be challenging to formulate full sentences for complex or heavily detailed topics on the fly.
- **It's limited to text.** The sentence method is of course all about sentences, and as such focuses completely on text. This means your notes may lack visual appeal and limit creative organization. Certain topics may be better suited to a more diagrammatic format, like mind maps.
- **It's limited to a hierarchical format.** This method, by virtue of the heading and sub-

heading format has obvious drawbacks if you need to be able to explore more complicated conceptual relationships between ideas and information.

**Verdict**: Overall, this method may work best for simple live lectures, and more complex textual reading like summarizing academic readings and reports. It's particularly useful if you want to get a clearer idea not only of the content, but of how that content is *structured*.

To decide if this approach is right for your project, consider what you could do with the finished notes. For example, you might listen to the video lecture on viruses and bacteria, taking notes in real time, then use those notes to create a quick summary for later review. Or, you might digest a series of articles and books about the Reformation, then use the notes to help you write a well-organized essay. The sentences you put down will help you shape the flow of your argument and inspire paragraph headings.

## **The Charting Method**

It's important to determine the level of organization and flexibility that you need before deciding on a note taking method. Let's look back at the virus and bacteria example: Imagine you need to learn a lot more about different types of infections. The information is no longer limited to comparing viruses and bacteria, now you have to look into other microorganisms like parasites as well.

Suddenly, the many variables and possible combinations are larger than can be neatly captured by the linear heading and sub-heading format. If you continued to use the sentence method, you would need to write long, awkward lists that repeat the same information, which would ultimately fail to reveal the underlying relationships connecting all these different pieces of data.

- Viruses, bacteria, and parasites differ in their interaction with the human or animal host body.
    - Viruses can't grow or reproduce outside a living cell, but can exist inertly on surfaces.
    - Bacteria can live and replicate outside the host body for hours or days.
    - Parasites cannot live or reproduce outside the host body.

You would have to repeat the above for every new point of comparison, leading to an extremely long and tedious list. There is a more intuitive and elegant way to organize this type of information, and it's something you've likely used throughout your life without realizing it: the charting method, which is also called the Matrix Method.

**The charting method has you organize data in a table, or matrix, with rows and columns.** This manner of organization condenses multiple relationships without repetition, so you can quickly understand everything at a glance. **Typically, each column corresponds to a category of some kind, and each row corresponds to a topic within that category**.

Naturally, this concept is easier to show than it is to explain in words. Below is a chart from a research paper published in the *International Journal of Academic Research in Business and Social Sciences* (Mohamed, 2019):

| Element/Company | Company A | Company B | Company C |
|---|---|---|---|
| Business Entry | Started as precast installer and later developed into onsite manufacturer | Started as IBS manufacturer from the beginning | Started as IBS manufacturer from the beginning |
| Business Positioning | Total solution provider to clients (design, manufacturing and installation) | Total solution provider to clients (design, manufacturing and installation) | Total solution provider to clients (design, manufacturing and installation) |
| Market Target | Public projects and targets large volume building components | Public and private projects and targets large volume building components | Public and private projects and targets large volume building components |
| Business Structure | Standalone entity with a small number of fulltime employees | Subsidiary of a large construction company with a small number of fulltime employees | Subsidiary of a large construction company with a small number of fulltime employees |
| Business Operation | In-house capability in design, manufacturing and installation, while outsourcing heavy machineries for onsite manufacturing and installation works. | In-house capability in design, manufacturing and installation with own mechanized factory, while outsourcing heavy logistics machineries | In-house capability in design, manufacturing and installation, while outsourcing heavy machineries for onsite manufacturing and installation works. |

Mohamed, Mohamed Rizal & Mohammad, Mohammad & Mahbub, Rohana & Gunasagaran, Sujatavani. (2019). Business Strategy of Small and Medium-Sized Enterprise Construction Companies in Adopting Industrialised Building System in Malaysia. *International Journal of Academic Research in Business and Social Sciences.* 9. 2222-6990. 10.6007/IJARBSS/v9-i9/6407.

As you can see, there are three columns for three categories: company A, B, and C. Each row then represents a different element of a company: Business entry, business positioning, market target, business structure, and business operation. A matrix like this helps highlight the intersections between the column and row values. This example allows us to see at a glance how companies A, B and C compare against one another in regards to different business elements.

The same thing can be seen below, in a chart from a paper titled, "The Rules of the Intergovernmental Game in East Asia: Decentralization Frameworks and Processes" (Smoke, 2005). Again, we can see the interplay between different categories of analysis (governmental system, political competition, etc.) and various countries (Cambodia, Chinea etc.):

| Country | Governmental system | Political competition | Legislative branch | Executive branch |
|---|---|---|---|---|
| Cambodia | Constitutional monarchy | Multiparty; Cambodia People's Party dominates | National Assembly and Senate with direct elections | King (head of state); prime minister (head of government) designated by National Assembly |
| China | Popular republic | Single party: Chinese Communist Party | National People's Congress elected by lower-level congresses | President, vice president, and state council (15 members, including prime minister) all designated by National People's Congress |
| Indonesia | Democratic republic | Competitive multiparty system | People's Assembly (DPR) directly elected; largely consultative Regional Representative Council (DPD) created in 2004; People's Consultative Assembly (MPR) composed of DPR and DPD manages constitutional reform | President elected by the People's Consultative Assembly until direct election in 2004 |
| Philippines | Democratic republic | Competitive multiparty system | House of Representatives and Senate largely directly elected | President elected directly by the people |
| Thailand | Constitutional monarchy | Multiparty: two dominate | Parliament with direct elections | King (head of state); prime minister (head of government) designated by Parliament |
| Vietnam | Popular republic | Single party: Vietnamese Communist Party | National Assembly elected by lower-level assemblies | President and state council (including prime minister) designated by National Assembly |

Smoke, P. (2005). The Rules of the Intergovernmental Game in East Asia: Decentralization Frameworks and Processes. *Political Science.*

Unlike the full sentences in the sentence method, here we use sentence fragments and small bits of factual or statistical information. That way, we can quickly compare and contrast ideas, and see broader themes emerge. What would require pages and pages of long-form text in the sentence method can be achieved with a small, data-packed diagram.

This method is so efficient at conveying its meaning that you can quickly understand the principle just by looking at it. Nevertheless, here is the step-by-step process to create matrices and tables the right way.

## Step 1: Identify your categories and your topics

Don't rush this step, since it might not be immediately obvious what your categories are, or how many of them there are. Depending on what you're trying to convey with your chart, it may be wiser to place the categories along the columns, or along the rows. For some kinds of data, it won't matter, but a good rule of thumb is that the smaller number of items is best plotted horizontally, onto columns. Then, even if you have many different topics for each category, you can simply make the table as long as necessary.

## Step 2: Create the chart

You can create a table in Microsoft Excel, in Word, or in Google docs, and you can easily adjust the columns, rows, headings, color shading, page orientation, and so on. Of course, there's nothing to stop you incorporating a quick sketched table into other notes, or drawing one carefully by hand.

**Step 3: Complete the chart**

Fill out each field with relevant notes, details, and summaries. Here, brevity is key, so stick to bullet points and short blurbs.

One of the great things about the charting method is that you fine-tune your own understanding as you go through the process of creating it. You also reinforce that understanding every time you review the chart, which acts as a neat summary and a study resource.

Here's one way to modify this method into a revision tool: After studying and memorizing your chart, print out an empty version, and challenge yourself to fill in each field from memory.

Pros and Cons

*The charting method excels where the sentence method falls short:*

- **It's data rich.** You can quickly represent factual or statistical information that would be too cumbersome to write down in full sentences.
- **It's efficient.** A table is quick to make up and takes up very little space. You cut out unnecessary details and focus on the salient parts only.
- **It shows relationships.** You don't just see the facts and data, but how that data combines, compares, or interacts with other data in a grid. This allows you to grasp bigger themes and patterns than if you had used a more linear way to represent your information.

*But it has its drawbacks:*

- **It's not good with subtlety.** You can easily compare single words or data points, but you may struggle to capture more nuanced ideas, such as those you'd find in philosophy or literature.

**Verdict:** The charting method is efficient and information dense. It is most useful when you have to quickly synthesize, summarize, and potentially compare large amounts of superficial data. However, if you find that your topic can't be neatly separated into 3 or more categories, or if you need space to explore significant depth and nuance in your note taking, this method will likely fall short.

## **Get the GIST**

Both the sentence method and the charting method assume that you know what information is important or relevant enough to be taken down in your notes. But what if you don't? **The GIST strategy is designed to help you identify the most important pieces of information, without bogging you down with detail and nuance.** It can help if you find yourself struggling to find the main, essential pieces of information, whether that's during a live lecture or when reading a text of some kind.

It may seem like a simple thing to just "identify the most important information," but in reality, it's not always obvious, and many of us are not skillful at reliably picking out the most important elements. You can prove this to yourself with a quick test: The next time you read something in a novel or textbook, stop, immediately shut the book, and see if you can quickly summarize what you have just read in 15 or 20 words, no more.

If you struggle to do this, it doesn't mean that you haven't properly grasped what you've read–but it does mean that unless you deliberately take the time to capture that information and condense it for yourself, your comprehension may continue to be shallow and fleeting.

The GIST strategy-Generating Interactions between Schemata and Text-is a useful tool to use when sifting out the most critical information in a text or lecture. The acronym was created in 1982 by James Cunningham, the professor emeritus of literacy studies at the University of North Carolina at Chapel Hill.

Originally, the model was about guiding students in reading comprehension, and helping them to *scaffold* their learning, first applying the technique to short texts and then practicing on longer and more complicated ones.

The process is simple:

**Step 1: Read the text**

When you're first trying out this method, you might like to follow the route taken by Cunningham's students and start small. Pick a few shorts pieces to practice with before trying your hand at more difficult texts, journal articles, or entire books. If necessary, read the text a few times.

**Step 2: Find the 5Ws and the H**

It can be difficult to know what counts as "key information," but it's easier if you stick to the 5Ws and the H:

- Who?
- What?
- When?
- Where?
- Why?
- How?

Not all of these will be applicable, but merely asking the questions will help you start focusing on the details that matter–and only those details.

**Step 3: Make your summary**

Using the information you identified in step 2, compile a summary of no more than 15 to 20 words. It's very important that you stick to this tight word count limit; being unable to meet it is often a sign that you're including irrelevant information, and this suggests that you haven't, in fact, identified the most important information. You may still be lacking a certain clarity about the *main* message of the text.

The 5Ws and the H concept is a perennial favorite of journalists, because it helps them "stick to the facts" and make sure they're not forgetting anything important. However, the summary is not just facts–you want the facts to connect meaningfully into a sentence that clearly outlines a cause-and-effect relationship or narrative.

For example, here is how you might summarize John Steinbeck's great American novel, *The Grapes of Wrath*:

- Who: the Joad family
- What: migrated
- When: 1929 - 1940
- Where: from Oklahoma to California
- Why: to survive the Great Depression

- How: bravely

GIST Summary: *The Joad family bravely migrated from Oklahoma to California to survive the Great Depression of the early 1900s.*

Of course, there is no way to truly summarize an entire novel, but this is the nature of the exercise: Can you look through any size text and quickly sift out the most key details? By using the GIST strategy, you should be able to arrive at a summary that instantly and uniquely identifies the text you have read, without missing any key details, and without adding anything superfluous.

This method, as with most of the techniques we'll explore in this book, is simple, but not necessarily easy. It is all too tempting to assume that you already know the basic facts and details, but until you sit down to sift your way through them step by step, you won't know just how thorough your understanding really is.

Working through each of the questions will keep you focused and help you identify any gaps in your comprehension and knowledge. For example, you might realize that although you understand plenty about the Great Depression, you're fuzzy on exact dates and locations. Likewise, when you explore the *why* of the story, you might find yourself facing many possible answers.

If you were summarizing *The Diary of Anne Frank*, for example, what would you note as the *why* of the text? Anne Frank hid in an attic and she wrote in a journal. But which of these two actions is most important? Depending on this answer, your answers to the other questions will change. For example, why did she hide in the attic? To escape Nazi persecution. Why did she write in her journal? As a way to cope.

The goal is not just to produce the "correct" summary, but to thoughtfully engage with your reading. In the example of Anne Frank, you might think it over a little and realize that both the hiding and the journaling are part of a broader attempt to survive a terrifying time in history (much like the Joad family in *Grapes of Wrath*).

Pros and Cons

*The GIST strategy has many benefits:*

**It's clarifying.** Rather than assuming that you've clearly grasped the fundamentals, the GIST strategy challenges you to prove your understanding by requiring you to give a clear, concise summary.

**It improves understanding.** It's not just about data points, but about how they connect, and the threads of logic or cause and effect that link them. It may seem like an easy task, but it will reinforce deeper comprehension.

**It supports revision.** You can use your summaries to review for tests, and quickly jog your memory about certain texts.

*The GIST strategy has very few drawbacks, but they need to be considered:*

**There are limits:** The bigger and more complicated the text, the more detail is lost in a 20 word summary. Summaries, by design are limited, but you may occasionally have a text that simply cannot be reduced this way. Trying to cram Tolstoy's *War and Peace* into 20 words, for example, is likely to yield a summary so broad and subjective as to be useless.

**Verdict:** Ideally, the GIST strategy works best for short- and medium-length texts, such as journal articles, reports, news, magazine articles, short stories, and the like. In fact, a GIST summary can be a way to both guide and review your reading of a complicated article. On your first skim reading, keep your eyes open for the Who, What, Where etc., and on your second more in-depth reading, craft your 20-word summary. You might like to attach this summary to the front of the paper so you can see the important details immediately. Such a summary will be invaluable if you're trying to synthesize many sources of information for a research project.

## Chunking Information

**Chunking information is simply the act of breaking large and complex pieces of information into smaller, more manageable chunks.** Chunking helps to reduce cognitive load, and it improves both our recall and our understanding.

The GIST strategy gives us a great example of chunking information. GIST requires that we carefully identify "the 5Ws and the H." This is a great example of chunking information!

Chances are that you can recall exactly what the 5Ws and the H stand for without having to go back and double check. We can do this because the information has been chunked– we don't have to remember the six items individually, but just three pieces of data: there are five questions, they all begin with W, and there is also an H.

Now, this is a very minor example, and most people would chunk the information this way automatically and intuitively. Yet the principle is sound, and can be truly impressive when applied to larger and more intimidating amounts of information.

Let's briefly consider the neuroscience behind the chunking concept. Research by George Armitage Miller in 1956 suggested that human short-term memory functions a little like a box with limited storage space–in fact, the title of the famous work was "The Magical Number Seven, Plus or Minus Two: Some Limits on Our Capacity for Processing Information." In this text, Miller explains how the brain can only cope with five to nine pieces of information at a time.

Chunking is essentially a kind of hack or cheat code given our hard-wired limitations. It's all about modifying information so that it is more easily and readily grasped by the short-term memory. There are three steps to follow when chunking information to make things simpler and easier to understand:

**Step 1: Simply break it down**

Slice the information into multiple, smaller pieces of information, making sure that the pieces still logically relate to one another if possible. For example, instead of remembering the phone number 8859734545, you can break it into pieces and remember 885 973 4545–which is closer to three chunks than it is to ten. It's a tiny difference, but it nevertheless eases the burden on your brain, and ultimately allows you to remember more.

**Step 2: Find connections and themes**

This is precisely what we did with the "5W and the H" example. We noticed what was common to each item (they all begin with W) and effectively condensed five pieces of data (who, what, where, when, and why) down into two: the 5 and the W. While you still do have to remember what each of the questions are, the 5W mnemonic provides you with a starting point that organizes your thinking, and cues your memory. The overall result is that your brain needs to do a tiny bit less work.

You can chunk information in this way by finding a pattern or repeating theme that connects two or more pieces of data into one. Look for relationships and connect things in meaningful ways. Is there a timeline, or a cause-and-effect process?

It's much easier for your brain to remember chains and webs of information than disparate items that don't connect in any way. For example, it's easier to remember a shopping list if you organize it first into separate categories (vegetables, red things, things needed to make breakfast etc.) than it is to remember each individual item.

**Step 3: Pull everything back together again**

Consider the periodic table. You could break this dense, information-heavy chart down into rows and columns, then create mnemonics and little stories to help you remember the characteristics of each group of elements. But then, you would likely also need to practice putting all those chunks back together again. You may need yet another chunk to be the key piece of information that helps you join things back up.

You could be studying the topic of the stages of photosynthesis by breaking a long process down into many smaller sub-processes, each organized by theme. However, you could also take care to add little "connectors" on either side of these chunks, so you know exactly where they fit into the bigger picture.

Breaking things down, seeking higher-order themes and links, and putting things back together sounds rather simple, but the magic comes when you find a way to apply these simple concepts to a work that is genuinely vast and overwhelming. Our examples here are necessarily simplified, but don't let that fool you–chunking can dramatically reduce the amount of work your brain has to do to grasp and absorb more complicated material.

Deconstruction

Deconstruction Follows the same process as chunking information, but it is about focused, targeted, and strategic information processing rather than about making things simpler or easier to understand. Your brain is not just a machine that you feed information to on a conveyor belt; it's a sophisticated organ that learns via genuine understanding. Thus, we can think of deconstruction as *meaningful chunking*.

When we deconstruct something, we follow the same process as when we chunk information, but we do so with a focus on the following questions:

**What do I need to learn?**

What is the goal you're trying to accomplish? This is not something vague, but very clear, specific, and concrete. "I want to learn about photosynthesis." is too vague. "I want to commit to memory these seven particular stages of photosynthesis, so that I can successfully recreate this diagram." is a better goal.

**Given my goal, how should I break things down?**

The way you break information down should not be arbitrary. In this example, there are several natural chunks for each stage of photosynthesis, which all ultimately feed into the final diagram. Each of these stages may be further broken down, but it is essential to do so in a way that makes sense, rather than just randomly slicing the process up.

## What is missing in my understanding or my recall?

Take a look at each chunk and identify those in which you may be lacking knowledge or comprehension. Perhaps you notice that you can recall the stages of photosynthesis, but you're stumbling when it comes to remembering how they fit together. Once you identify a deficiency in your comprehension, go and deliberately fill in those gaps. Read up, research, ask for help, or engage in repeat practice.

## How can I synthesize everything and test myself?

After you've drilled the missing information a few times, test your learning by making yourself reconstruct the diagram again, according to the chunks and mnemonics you set up for yourself. Sit down with a pen and paper and attempt to draw the diagram from memory–not just remembering the information, but truly grasping the cause-and-effect sequence they're all a part of. You may need to repeat steps 3 and 4 a few times to gain mastery. Utilizing this process will allow you to focus on the pieces that still require your attention, instead of wasting time on excessive or irrelevant information, or things you already understand.

Pros and Cons

*Chunking/deconstruction has many benefits:*

**It's widely applicable.** Almost every conceivable topic can be broken down and deconstructed to improve understanding.

**It improves memory.** By utilizing information chunking and tools like mnemonics to reduce cognitive load, you make it easier for your short-term memory to retain more information.

**It's adaptable.** There are countless ways to use the principle of chunking, and the method can be endlessly modified to suit any need.

*Chunking/deconstruction is a part of most study and note taking methods, but it has one key disadvantage*:

**It cannot correct misunderstanding.** Chunking improves memory and recall, but if you've fundamentally misunderstood something, chunking may not reveal your error or give you the opportunity to correct it.

**Verdict:** There's pretty much no reason *not* to use some form of chunking or deconstruction in your note taking. While these methods can seem blindingly obvious when we consider them in terms of what we already know, they can be astoundingly clarifying when navigating our way through material that we are *not* yet familiar with. After all, life's most complex topics don't come neatly pre-chunked; instead, it is our deliberate attempt to discover and delineate those chunks that actually allows us to meaningfully grasp what we're examining.

**Summary:**

- All note taking requires some very basic "nuts and bolts" practical skills, such as chunking and deconstruction, summarizing, or organizing incoming data using techniques like the sentence method or the charting method.

- With the sentence method, we clearly separate out new ideas, thoughts, and themes into full sentences that each have their own line. As we add to these sentences, we gain a precisely organized and comprehensive view of the information we're taking in.
- With the charting method, we organize data into columns and rows to create a matrix, with the columns corresponding to a category of some kind, and the rows corresponding to a topic within that category. Not only is this concise and efficient, it also clearly shows relationships between data pieces.
- The GIST strategy (Generating Interactions between Schemata and Text) helps you identify what's most important. We read the text, find the 5Ws and the H, then generate a concise 15-20-word summary. Summaries can be used to improve comprehension and recall.
- Information chunking and deconstruction help us improve understanding and

retention. We first break information down into more manageable and meaningful chunks, then condense that information by identifying links and themes, and finally practice by putting everything back together again.

Chapter Two: Thinking in Hierarchies to Get Organized

Getting organized is not just a matter of practicality or ease; if we hope to take notes that accurately reflect the structure and organization of the things we're learning about, then our note taking itself needs to be well-structured and organized.

Learning to "think in hierarchies" means learning to see the inherent structure and order in things. In this chapter we are paying attention to note taking methods that reveal the underlying organization of what we're learning, and at the same time train us to think in more logical, ordered and structured ways.

### **Mind Mapping**

Mind maps are instantly recognizable, and you've probably had plenty of experience creating them during your school days. Very simply, **a mind map is a method of organizing and visualizing data in such a way as to highlight certain hierarchies and relationships**.

Mind maps are best when used as organizational tools that help you clarify and understand the interconnections within a complex main theme. They are an intuitive note taking tool, but their simplicity is deceptive, and many people waste time creating mind maps that are *visually* appealing, but lack organizational power.

In this section, we'll be focusing on the ability of a mind map to both shape and represent your thought process, not aesthetically, but hierarchically. As you create the mind map, you are formalizing and clarifying a concept in your mind Once the mind map is created, you have a permanent visual reminder of that concept, which you can use for study and review.

Below we'll look at the basic technique for creating mind maps that really work, with some examples. Bear in mind that the way you put together your own mind maps depends heavily on your purpose; you can use mind maps for open-ended brainstorming, to take notes during a live lecture, to keep track of certain elements as you gather research, or to plan essays and assignments.

**Step 1: Clarify the main topic**

Of course, the main topic is the center point of the mind map. This could be a theme or idea, but it can also be a question or an aim/goal. You can draw a square or circle in the middle of the page and label it with your main topic. "How to plan a bid for funding" or "Main themes in Dostoevsky's work," for example.

**Step 2: Branch off with subtopics**

Decide on the subcategories of the main topic and branch them off from the center. Typically, if you imagine the mind map as a clock face, you'd put the first subtopic at 1 o'clock and continue in a clockwise direction. For the Dostoevsky mind map, for example, you could identify a few main themes to branch off: "poverty," "the human condition," "the Russian Orthodox Church," "free will," "the father-son relationship," "suicide," and so on.

For the topic of bid writing, you could list "executive summary," "budget," "compliance information," etc. What's important is that your visual depiction of topic and subtopic actually makes sense, and is a true representation of a hierarchical relationship that actually exists.

Consider coding additional information in the style of the branches. For example, a thick/dark branch might suggest a strong relationship, while a thin or dashed line represents a more tenuous connection. Use color and symbols to convey extra information, for example using a red line to denote an adversarial relationship between concepts. You can use proximity to the central point to depict importance or occurrence in time; for example, very important events could be central, while tangential ones are spread on the periphery.

**Step 3: Keep adding further branches**

Off of these you can add more branches to denote further conceptual subdivisions. These subdivisions could be smaller categories, examples, supporting ideas, premises of an argument, or relevant details. For example, off the branch "Russian Orthodox Church," you could draw additional branches, "conversion," "sin and redemption," and so on.

Naturally, you can branch off as many times as necessary, but usually even the most complex topics can be expressed neatly on a single page. The trick is knowing when to add detail and when to stop! In the same way as we worked to identify the underlying structure and logic of arguments in a previous section, Here we are compiling a visual representation of structure, i.e., the broad connections and relationships between a topic and its subtopics.

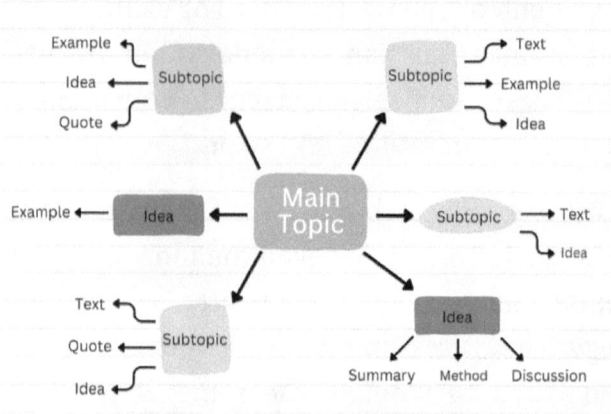

*Image from https://subjectguides.york.ac.uk*

Pros and Cons

*Mind maps are a common note taking strategy that have many benefits:*

**They represent hierarchy.** Mind maps are most effective at representing concepts that possess some degree of natural hierarchy, or layered relationships and connections.

**They can handle larger concepts.** They work well for depicting larger concepts that can be broken down into smaller components. With the flexibility of using as many branches as necessary, they allow you to cover complex relationships and connections within a topic.

**They are creative and flexible.** You can use any number of tricks to visually represent the connections within a mind map. A thick red line can indicate something completely different from a dashed green line, giving you more detail and nuance without taking up extra space.

*While mind maps have very strong benefits, they do have a couple significant downfalls:*

**They represent hierarchy.** The purpose of a mind map is to visualize complex, layered relationships between subtopics. They are less effective for concepts where this hierarchy doesn't actually exist. If your topic doesn't have layered connections, or if all of the information you need falls on a single level, a mind map won't offer usable insights.

**They can struggle to hold fine detail.** Mind maps are not good at holding lots of fine detail and, the more complex the topic, the more you will have to simplify it in order to make a mind map. This simplification might help to an extent, but there may be a point at which the map is too simplified to be of any use.

Verdict: Mind maps are great for visualizing complex relationships and connections between a main topic and several subtopics. By virtue of their design, they offer great creative flexibility for including detail without taking up a lot of space. They do struggle with fine detail, and can over-simplify to the point of being unhelpful. Finally, mind maps are great for drilling and revising, and can help improve retention and recall. One great idea is to create a mind map, study it, and then later challenge yourself to recreate it from memory, paying close attention not just to the content, but to the way the content interconnects.

An important thing to note: Mind maps are quite labor intensive to create. The mind map is meant to help you clarify relationships and connections, but you'll struggle to draw a good mind map if you don't already understand those connections and relationships. Editing mind maps as you go might help you slowly fill in the gaps, but again, this takes time that you might not have.

For these reasons, mind maps are best used to summarize and condense information already known and gathered, so that you can commit it to memory and practice your recall. For example, take notes during a live lecture, then later review those notes and create a mind map to summarize the material on one page. Before an exam, use the mind map you made to quickly jog your memory.

## **The QEC Method**

**The QEC (Questions, Evidence, Conclusion) Method is an extremely useful tool for organizing information in non-technical subjects, particularly those in the arts and humanities.** Learning expert and author of *How to Become a Straight A Student* Cal Newport claims that this approach is his go-to note taking strategy for non-technical topics.

The QEC Method is a way of expressing big ideas and concepts by compiling structured summaries. It's especially useful for any information that contains a thread of argument or a linear narrative structure, such as history, philosophy, and literature. Like many of the methods explored in this book, the QEC method can be used in both directions, i.e., as a way to help digest and process texts and also a way to plan and organize your own texts like essays or answers to exam questions.

The steps to the QEC process are simple:

**Step 1: Question**

List out some questions inspired by your textbook, headings and subheadings, lecture learning objectives, mock exams, or simply your own curiosity.

**Step 2: Evidence**

Set out to find the answers to your question by reading and researching.

**Step 3: Conclusion**

Gather the evidence that you've found and condense your findings into a simple summary statement that answers the initial question.

Consider the example below, which comes from the University of Toronto Scarborough's *Learning Strategies* webpage. Let's say you start with a focused question, "How does endurance training increase maximal oxygen uptake (VO2max)?" To help you find the answer to this question, you decide to read a paper with a promising title: "Effect of Endurance Training on Parameters of Aerobic Fitness."

| Question | Evidence | Conclusion |
|---|---|---|
| How does endurance training increase maximal oxygen uptake (VO2max)?<br><br>VO2max = max amount of oxygen body can use during exercise | 1) Elite endurance athletes have high cardiac output which increases VO2max<br>  o Higher cardiac output = more blood & more oxygen delivered to muscles<br><br>2) Exercising muscle able to extract more O2 due to increase in # of capillaries | Endurance training causes adaptations in the cardiovascular system via increasing cardiac output (delivery of O2) and increasing skeletal muscle's capability to extract O2 from the blood |

Utoronto.ca. (2025). *QEC Method | Learning Strategies*. [online] Available at: https://www.utsc.utoronto.ca/learningstrategies/qec-method [Accessed 25 Jan. 2025].

You read this paper in a deliberate and strategic way, searching for the answers to your question, and you do indeed find answers. You note these down and then condense that information into a conclusion. As you can see above, arranging your questions and answers into a QEC table is a neat way to not only process new information, but also mark your key learning moments. You can extend this table to include as many rows as you have questions, and over time you will have a record of your growing development and learning.

The power of the QEC approach is that it structures your endeavors around the most obvious center: curiosity about what you don't yet know. This keeps you focused and actively engaged at the very limits of your understanding, rather than wasting time rehashing what you already know.

The QEC method is also a great way to develop your ability to think in hierarchies. If you look closely, many of your questions and answers will reveal fundamental relationships and their hidden structure and order. You can imagine that each question is a branch out of the central point on a mind map, and the answers are the further branches that stem off of each question. Let's consider in more detail how to run through the QEC process.

**Step 1: Devise a question**

Questions are always a good idea, but not all questions are created equal. Recall that the QEC method is ideal for high level concepts and big ideas, such as those in history, philosophy, and literature. This means that the best questions will be those that can help you uncover or clarify a certain argument or narrative structure, rather than just queries about factual data.

The most productive questions look like this:

*What were the main factors leading up to the industrial revolution?* (History)

*In what ways did neurologist Jean-Martin Charcot influence the development of Freud's theories?* (Psychology)

*What economic events inspired the boom of "J horror" in Japan during the late 1980s and early 1990s?* (Film, media studies)

These questions are ideal because they are neither too broad nor too narrow. For topics that possess a kind of internal argumentative structure, these questions will help you understand how various premises support a final conclusion. The right questions will encourage deeper reflection on the topic, as well as help you develop more structured and hierarchical thinking.

**Take the time to properly formulate your questions.** If you intend to use the QEC method to take notes during a live class or lecture, then a big clue will be the title of the lecture, or else the headings of any prescribed readings. If you want to use the method to help structure your own thinking, you might find it illuminating to begin with all the aspects of a topic you are still unclear about. You can also find ideas for good questions by looking at exam questions, essay topics, or reading materials that are explicitly set up as question-and-answer dialogues.

### Step 2: Look for evidence

Next, get to work answering your question by finding evidence. Use bullet points and keywords to be brief so you don't get lost in the details. Let's continue with the example of the question "What were the main factors leading up to the industrial revolution?" We could note down the following points, either in real time during a lecture, or during a more open-ended brainstorming session:

- Britain had natural resources like coal and iron
- Invention of steam trains and existing transport network
- Population boom
- Colonial trade
- Relative political stability
- Pool of entrepreneurs, excess labor, investment capital
- Etc.

Step 3: Write a conclusion

The final step is to summarize all the evidence you've gathered into a concise conclusion that answers your initial question. Depending on the complexity of your question, you may need to weigh various premises and competing lines of argument, or you may simply need to synthesize the main points and condense them into a single answer.

In our example, we can come to the following conclusion: *The industrial revolution was made possible by a confluence of certain political, economic, and cultural changes in Britain. European imperialist growth and advances in agriculture and technology allowed for the emergence of industrial capitalism.*

Of course, such a summary is going to be simplified and broad–much like the summaries we created using the GIST method. But this summary can be extremely useful:

- It can help you generate further questions and reveal aspects you are still unclear about. For example, which came first, the invention of the steam engine, or the revolution in the iron industry? How exactly did that work?
- It can serve as a memory aid for study and review.
- It can help you keep track of your progress, i.e., what you understand, and what you are still trying to understand.

As you can imagine, the QEC method can be creatively combined with other approaches covered in this book; the defining characteristic of this method, however, is the use of questions and answers to gradually reveal underlying structure.

## The 80/20 Rule or Pareto Principle

**The Pareto principle describes a universal pattern in which a small portion (20%) of causes account for a large proportion (80%) of effects.** It takes its name from Italian economist Vilfredo Pareto, who noted that around 80% of Italy's land was owned by 20% of its residents. Later in 1941, management consultant Joseph Juran took this observation and applied it to his own field of engineering, noting that 20% of defects caused 80% of problems. Today the Pareto principle has been expanded and given many more names, including the 80/20 rule, or "the law of the vital few."

The Pareto principle is what is called a "power law" in mathematics, and describes a kind of disproportionate distribution of causes and effects that can be seen in many natural phenomena, such as:

- 20% of your efforts might produce 80% of your results
- 20% of customers generate 80% of online reviews

- 20% of a company's workers produce 80% of company profit
- 20% of dissatisfied customers require 80% of customer service time
- 20% of a book represents 80% of its total value

This is a *principle*, however, so the numbers will not be exactly 80 and 20. What's important is the disproportionate distribution, and what this means for our learning in general, and our note taking in particular.

The big idea is to focus on what is most important, most impactful, and most decisive. We have limited time, energy, and resources, so it makes sense that we allocate these things to tasks and ideas that will bring us the most reward. Ultimately, it's a question of efficiency.

Sometimes, note taking fails because the note-taker is a kind of perfectionist, who unfortunately wastes time trying to comprehensively capture each and every detail they encounter. This is a wasteful approach, since not every piece of information is weighed equally. Instead, when taking notes, we should focus on those high-yield, impactful areas *first*.

**Step 1: Identify the high yield areas**

Before you even begin note taking, brainstorming, or planning out an essay, survey what's ahead of you and **try to identify the 20%.**

What tasks, ideas, components, topics, themes, etc. are the ones that, if mastered or undertaken, would give you the biggest payoff? If 20% of your customers are generating 80% of your online reviews, then make satisfying those customers your priority. If 20% of the book contains 80% of its value, then put most of your effort into understanding and applying that 20%, and don't worry so much about the rest.

Identifying what is most important is not as easy as you'd think, but there are always a few hints. Notice what your lecturer or tutor repeatedly focuses on, or what they start with. Notice the most emphasized ideas in the titles, headings, and summaries available to you. Bear in mind also that what is considered important is often relative; consider your own goals and tasks and use that as your yardstick.

**Step 2: Identify high-yield approaches**

It may be that the relevant 20% is *content-based* (for example, you need to focus on chapter 5 most of all, or prioritize the circulatory system over the reproductive system) or it might be *method or process based* (for example you need to pay most attention to learning to solve essay type questions, or master a certain reading skill over another). In real life, you'll typically need to focus on both!

High yield note taking approaches are always *focused* and *active* by nature. If you get stuck passively reading and re-reading, you're not going to get as much from the material than if you'd engaged more actively and strategically. This is exactly what the approaches covered in this book are intended to do. However, the magic lies not in the techniques themselves, but in their applicability to the topic at hand. In other words, we have to actively decide for ourselves what is "high yield" on a case-by-case basis.

**Step 3: Adjust as you go**

You might not be perfectly accurate in your assessment of what is most important the first time around–and that's OK. Take any relevant feedback and adjust your approach and your area of focus accordingly. For example, in preparation for a midterm exam you may have spent most of your time studying chapter 5, creating summaries and mind maps. In the exam, however, you notice that even though chapter 5 material is disproportionately represented, so is chapter 6, which you didn't spend as much energy on. You make a note of this so that you are better prepared for the final exam.

Another thing to consider is that the most important 20% may change over time. This means that we need to be ready to adapt, constantly asking whether our strategy is getting us the results we want. We can even apply the 80/20 principle to the 80/20 principle itself, and ask, "What parts of my 80/20 rule implementation have actually yielded the most results?"

**Using the Pareto principle for study sessions**

The three-step process above can be applied at many different levels, and on many different scales. On a simple level, you can use the Pareto principle to shape your study sessions or lectures:

1. Set a goal for what you hope to achieve after the session.
2. Quickly identify the priorities you'll focus on (*roughly* 20%).
3. Choose an active and engaged ("high yield") study technique appropriate to the task at hand.
4. At the end of the session, check in with your goal and evaluate your own performance. Essentially, you want to confirm that 80% of your progress and results for the session have indeed come from the 20% you identified in step 2.

**Using the Pareto principle for reading**

Written texts follow the 80/20 distribution: The key ideas represent a small proportion, and they will be expanded on and supported by a less important 80%. Pareto-inspired reading, therefore, is reading for the 20%; i.e., reading with the focused intention of identifying the most relevant details. To read for the 20%:

1. Scan the text, look at headings and layout, and try to get a sense of overall structure and argument. Identify the place where the main argument is likely to be set out.
2. Start your reading, but begin where you think the most important parts are, and engage with these ideas actively.
3. Do more in-depth reading of these important sections, perhaps making summaries, diagrams, and so on.
4. Scan through the rest of the text, looking for ways to fill in any gaps or provide more context; don't spend too long on it.

Overall, the Pareto principle is an *observation* about effort and its results in the world. When we understand the principle, then we can adopt a whole new attitude about how we work and study, and even how we think.

For example, instead of wasting an hour aimlessly working on a task, we first spend 10 minutes thinking strategically about how to approach it., Then, with intent and focus, we can spend our time on it much more efficiently. Instead of spending two hours reading ten different articles in detail, we spend just one hour gaining a fuller understanding of just three articles–but they're the most important three. The details here don't matter; what matters is that we are consistently able to ask ourselves, "What is most important here? What is the best use of my effort towards it?"

## **Knowledge Organization with Zettelkasten**

In today's information-soaked digital landscape, it's easy to become overwhelmed. The trouble is, trying to sift through information by taking notes can itself become part of the overwhelm. We may find ourselves drowning in bits of paper, half-read books, several dozen open yet unread tabs on our web browsers, random scribbles, bookmarks, highlighted journals…

We need to be organized! While the previous methods we've explored have focused on organizing our own learning and thought processes, the final method we'll explore is a practical one to keep track of the literal bits and pieces of information we inevitably generate on any learning journey.

This is the method called "Zettelkasten" which simply means "note box" in German. **A Zettelkasten is a place where you store all relevant pieces of information, often put on small note cards or papers.** First created by German sociologist Niklas Luhmann, the method is a popular data-management strategy, whether that data is academic research or material supporting your personal or intellectual development.

Luhmann was an advocate for ongoing and permanent note taking, where relevant pieces of information were captured the very moment they were encountered. By carefully processing and organizing these pieces of information, Luhmann was able to produce more than 70 books and 400 articles in his lifetime.

This caliber of note taking requires organizing information efficiently. It's a two-way relationship: Organizing scattered thoughts into a structured system enhances our understanding and recall, but the more organized we are in our own thinking, the more this will be reflected in the quality of the notes we keep. We can imagine that an organization system for our notes is a kind of secondary brain; the constant finetuning and adjustments we make to our *external* notes as we organize and reorganize them actually represents our ongoing *internal* development.

The Zettelkasten method is simple: we capture our ideas, concepts, themes, etc. individually, but then link them together into a whole so that over time we can discover broader patterns of interconnection. The idea is to construct a web or network, where each node is a piece of information we have. Seeing information in this big-picture way makes it easier to memorize, and to uncover new insights you never appreciated before.

Compared to mind mapping, summaries, and other more discrete note taking methods, the Zettelkasten approach has the capacity to organize vast amounts of complex information over the long term–even across the course of your life, should you wish it!

You can use this approach to manage material for a multi-year degree, for long-term creative ventures, for large research projects, or even for establishing interdisciplinary links. The web you create will be a dynamic, living thing that grows over time and is constantly evolving along with you as you increase in knowledge. You can think of a mature Zettelkasten system as your own personal wiki or library.

There is a learning curve with Zettelkasten, and you need to give yourself time to find your feet. Firstly, consider the types of notes or "Zettels":

- **Fleeting Notes:** Quick ideas captured on the go. They're not permanent, and are meant to be refined at a later point.

- **Literature Notes:** Notes taken from texts. One note is one idea (i.e., not a summary).

- **Permanent Notes**: These represent your long term, "banked" knowledge base. These ideas are fully expanded and established, and they connect to other permanent notes in the web.

- **Reference Notes**: A way to track metadata, i.e., information about the connections between notes, often in the form of a "tag", digital or not.

To understand how these four types of notes come together, consider the following step-by-step flow when starting and maintaining your Zettelkasten:

## Step 1: Capture the information

Let's say you're attempting to complete a basic science course and have decided to compile a Zettelkasten to organize the new information you're being exposed to.

As you're working through your course, you end up reading a piece about Newton's laws of motion. You recognize one especially relevant idea in a paragraph, and quickly note it down, writing, "Newton's First Law: An object in motion stays in motion unless acted upon by an external force." The unique identifier for this note is "001-Newton1." This is an example of a *literature note.*

When something catches your attention in a lecture, you spot something in a video, you hear someone mention something, or you catch a reference in a news story, you'll take down more notes. The individual notes that you make in the moment from each of these sources ends up as a *fleeting note*, waiting to be refined at some later date.

**Step 2: Organize your notes**

At some point, you need to consolidate all these fleeting and literature notes. This means going back through them and polishing the concepts and ideas into something more substantial. You may find yourself combining certain concepts and notes into one (for example, when you encounter Newton's second and third laws you can expand and rename your original note to 001-Newton, which now contain three smaller notes: 001-Newton1, 001-Newton2, 001-Newton3). This new note, with all of Newton's laws fully expanded on it, is called a *permanent note*.

You may also start to see how certain fleeting notes connect to other fleeting notes. For example, you read something interesting about friction, and so you add to your original note 001-Newton something like, "Friction acts as an external force that can stop motion." You then create a note to track all of your notes related to basic physics, like "Ref-Physics." This is a *reference note*.

**Step 3: Connect**

To start building an interconnected network, you need to identify and formalize links between notes. Make sure that you are using symbols, hyperlinks, or well-organized tags to keep track. These days, there is a wealth of technology available to help you do this digitally.

While working on your Newton notes, for example, you may realize that "001-Newton" links conceptually with a note you made earlier on Galileo's experiments. You formally create a link between them, tagging both with "Physics-History" so you can easily navigate between related ideas. Now, not only have you clarified this specific relationship, but you've created a dedicated place for all similar physics/history links to go.

**Step 4: Review**

The Zettelkasten is not a fixed object that you compile and forget. Rather, you regularly check in with it to update the information stored there, to refine or even delete certain notes, and to discover and clarify new patterns and connections.

In our example, you may discover a month later, while reviewing your "Ref-Physics" note, that you have a gap in your understanding, and don't yet know how Newton's laws influenced modern engineering. You add a new note titled "Modern Impact of Newton's Laws" and link it back to "001-Newton." This is a link that you might not have seen otherwise.

**Step 5: Apply**

You will undoubtedly gain fresh insights as you build and organize your Zettelkasten, but it's also worth taking the time to deliberately use it to generate new ideas and plan new projects or creations. Many months later you might be asked to submit a paper on the history of scientific breakthroughs.

Luckily for you, you have been diligently compiling a sophisticated Zettelkasten system that has already done a large amount of the work for you. You consult it and find that you can easily pull notes about Newton, Galileo, and a host of other inventors that connect to one another in unique and interesting ways.

You discover that your saved notes and their interconnections already form the structure of an essay, as well as spur you to think of other topics that might have otherwise evaded you.

**Summary:**

- A mind map is a method of organizing and visualizing data in a way that highlights certain hierarchies and relationships. Start with a main topic then add details with branching topic and subtopics to represent the bigger organizing structure. They are less suited for live lecture note taking, or for complex topics that don't possess a natural hierarchy.
- The QEC Method is a tool for organizing information in non-technical subjects, such as history, philosophy, or literature; the acronym stands for Question, Evidence, and Conclusion. This is a way of refining and tracking your learning through the power of questions you generate and answer yourself.
- The Pareto principle, or 80/20 rule, points to a universal pattern in which a small portion of causes account for a large proportion of effects. In both learning and

note taking, we need to focus on what is most important, most impactful, and most decisive.
- The Zettelkasten method helps us be effective note-takers over the long-term, allowing us a system that encourages efficiently organized information. A Zettelkasten is a dynamic network of organized and interconnected notes.

## Chapter Three: Strengthen Your Reading Comprehension

Chances are that most of your note taking will be focused on reading, whether that's textbooks, journal articles, new stories, reports, or novels. In this chapter, we'll be exploring a handful of techniques proven to improve reading comprehension.

Almost everyone in the modern Western world can read, but fewer of us are skilled at reading comprehension, and even less have mastered the art of truly engaged, critical thinking about what we read. This chapter will explore ways to develop that special set of skills that makes the difference between mere *reading* and actual *understanding*.

### **Effective Highlighting**

Highlighting as a study technique is so ubiquitous that many of us will reach for a highlighter to mark a textbook without thinking about what we're doing, or why. Despite its popularity, research shows that the wrong kind of highlighting does little to enhance your learning (Dunlosky, 2013). In fact, lazy highlighting may even create a false sense of understanding, and impair, rather than enhance, your comprehension.

What, then, is the *right* way to highlight?

It's no surprise: **effective highlighting requires deep, intentional engagement.** This is a subtle, but important point. Our highlighting needs to be a reflection of the way we are comprehending and working with a text; the mere dragging of a highlighter across a page will *not* in itself lead to that comprehension.

AP Psychology lecturer Blake Harvard explains it perfectly when he says that highlighting should be the beginning of learning, not the end. On his fantastic blog, *The Effortful Educator*, he explains that "There's not a lot of thinking involved with the use of highlighters; therefore, there's not a lot of learning." Highlighting is most effective when combined with other approaches that continually activate your brain getting you to interact meaningfully with what you're reading.

Below are three quick strategies for bringing more brainpower to the highlighting habit.

## Strategy 1: The brain-book-buddy approach

Just because you've highlighted something doesn't mean you've understood it or "learned" it in any way. Likewise, just because you've singled out something as important, it doesn't mean that it *is* important, or that you are more likely to find this piece of information in an exam, for example. You glance at a colorful page that looks as though it's been processed, but this is an illusion. It will only be processed when you process it!

The brain-book-buddy approach breaks you out of rote behaviors and uses highlighting to reveal gaps in knowledge, making you a more purposeful and focused reader. Instead of the illusory feeling of progress you get from seeing your pages increasingly marked up with color, use your highlighters to draw your attention to everything you *don't* know.

Here's how to do it: divide a sheet of paper into three columns: brain, book, and buddy. In the first column, challenge yourself to answer a question (perhaps from a mock test) without consulting any resources, i.e., use your *brain*. In this column, highlight in green what you're not 100% sure about. Then go and check these answers using notes and textbooks (use your *books*), and use the second column to add to or correct the answers you put down in the first, using a yellow highlighter. The final column is where you use your *buddy*, i.e., a friend or fellow student against whose answers you can compare your own. Together with your buddy, write down your final answer, using an orange or pink highlighter to mark the additional material that makes the answer the best it can be. Granted, you may not always have the luxury of a willing peer, but the principle remains.

All on one page, you can now visually track your process of improvement–not unlike the

QEC method discussed earlier. The first column gives you a clear idea of your performance without any further engagement, and from there you can see how your performance and comprehension has improved.

## Strategy 2: Creative annotations

When you highlight, your inner talk will usually be: "This matters, I'll emphasize this." But on later review, you might discover just how little impact this addition of color has really made. *Why* is it important? What does this highlight *mean,* relative to the rest of the page? Highlighting alone usually can't tell you. Merely memorizing something or being aware that it is important will not grant you a depth understanding.

For deeper, more critical engagement, we will need to experiment with the richer and more varied world of annotations. Remember that unless you actively engage with material by elaborating on it, explaining it, linking it with something else, or representing it symbolically, then the default for your brain is to forget it.

What are some good ways to annotate? The answer is: Whatever helps you engage. Some ideas:

- Include colors, symbols, little drawings and sketched diagrams, speech bubbles, punctuation marks, or other signs and codes to help you process what you're reading. For example, you could literally draw a line from one paragraph to another, scribble a confused face in the margins to symbolize a learning gap, or use a code to reference back to some other page, concept, or idea.
- "Dialogue" with the text–write your questions, responses, arguments, agreements, or predictions as you read. Imagine the author is talking to you, and pause now and again to paraphrase, clarify, or note your own response.
- Be creative. You can use stickers, little page tabs, different kinds of pens and markers, and other forms of visual representation. Your imagination really is the limit. If a peer is available, compare annotations and see what you can learn from one another's process.

## Strategy 3: Self-generated questions

Highlighting gives a false sense of completion and comprehension. You may feel that you've covered certain ground and then, when faced with a question in an exam, suddenly realize that your grasp of the material was only superficial.

Turn this tendency on its head by using highlighting to *generate questions*. As you read, pause and turn the information over in your head. Transform it into a question, and if it's a fundamental one, write it down for later revision. Your questions can be basic and factual, or they can be more complex. They can reflect what you already know, or the things you're genuinely not clear on yet.

This approach is a little like the QEC technique, but on a smaller scale. You might pause after each paragraph, for example, and turn the information you've highlighted into a question. Before reading on, answer that question in your own words, or use Feynman's approach (explored later in the book) to explain it in simple, non-jargon language. When you're done reading, you will have compiled a list of questions that you can use for review, or else expand on them using the full QEC approach if you're still unclear on the answers.

## **Active Listening and Note Taking**

In the same way that highlighting can become automatic and superficial, so can listening. While reading a text, we can pause now and then to process what we're taking in, participating mentally with the new material, rather than passively letting it wash by. Why not bring the same spirit to listening?

We need to develop ears that can recognize key information as we hear it, so that we are able to mentally highlight it and tell ourselves, "Aha, this is important." Active listening will, of course, be a more dynamic process than active reading, and demands enough energy and intention to consistently notice and pull out those crucial details in real time.

If you find that live lectures are difficult for you, then this may suggest there is room for improvement in the skill of active listening. The first step is to understand that listening is never a passive process, where we simply sit, like empty containers, and try to catch as much as we can. Instead, engaged and focused listening expends enormous amounts of energy to *internalize* new information.

But here's a surprise. The biggest problem with listening to lectures is not that they are overwhelming or too fast; the biggest risk is that we actually find them too slow and boring. It seems counterintuitive, but lectures and lessons delivered orally may actually be under-stimulating. There is some evidence that people process their own thoughts up to four times as fast as someone can deliver those thoughts through speech. Author of the bestseller *Persuasion: The Art of Influencing People* James Borg claims that people speak on average 120–150 words per minute, but think at 600–800 words per minute.

Whether these precise figures are correct or not, this discrepancy has two important implications: Firstly, it means that we may often find ourselves bored and distracted, and our focus may wane. Secondly, it reminds us that if we *can* maintain focus, there are huge untapped cognitive resources ready at our disposal.

With active listening, let's imagine that we are listening four times as intently. You pay higher quality attention (and more of it) to additional non-verbal channels of information you may otherwise ignore, such as body language, tone of delivery, and the bigger message that is being offered.

What is the structure of the argument being presented? Can you spot the main premises, the rhetoric being used, the evidence, the quality of the evidence, the important details, and the not-so-important details?

The more of this you can "read" into an oral lesson, the deeper and more thoroughyour comprehension will be–and the less boring you'll find it! What's more, you'll be simultaneously engaging your critical thinking, so as you take in new information, you're also appraising and evaluating it.

Below are some practical strategies for cultivating this kind of active listening mindset within yourself.

### Set the stage

Focus is not just a cognitive act; it's also something we do with our environment. By creating environments that allow us to devote our full attention to the topic at hand, you are focusing yourself. Turn off your phone, get rid of anything that might disrupt you, and adopt a comfortable posture that won't distract you. Imagine a tunnel opening up that directly connects the lecturer's mouth and your brain, and imagine everything outside that tunnel fading away to irrelevance.

Take the attitude that the lecturer is about to share with you the most important and fascinating thing you've ever heard in your life–be *that* intentional and attentive. While you wait for the lecture to begin, mentally review previous material or note any predictions or questions you have about the upcoming lecture. Bring appropriate pens and notebooks, and most importantly, bring presence, respect, and attention to the process.

**Prick your ears for discourse markers**

When reading, you can visually see the way the author has structured their message by looking at headings and subheadings. In a live lecture, however, the trick is to learn to hear these "auditory headings," and pay attention to what they're trying to tell you. **Discourse markers are little indicators that the speaker uses to tell you that they consider something important.** Look for verbs like *talk* or *explore* as well as words indicating importance, such as *main*, *key,* or *principle*. For example:

- "Now I want to *share* something *important* with you..."
- "The *key* thing I want to *say* is..."
- "The *main topic* we're *investigating* today..."
- "Today's *discussion*..."

When written down, such markers seem fairly obvious, but they are surprisingly easy to miss when spoken in real time, especially if we're not really paying attention. If you hear these markers, stay alert–what follows is likely a main idea.

There are countless other discourse markers, too. For example, the following phrases indicate that a formal definition is about to be offered, and this is usually something you'll want to note. Listen for phrases like:

- "...is defined as,"

- "...is said to be,"
- "...is known as,"
- "...is widely known as,"

If you hear something like "three things" or "five different kinds," then scribble down a little mind map or simply be alert to the fact that you are being told something about structure and components. If you hear "to repeat," "again," or "to reiterate," you are being told loud and clear that what follows is important.

If you hear words like "advantage," "drawback," "benefit," "pros and cons," etc., then prime yourself to hear an evaluation of the topic, or a comparison between two topics. You may even ready yourself to draw a little table or mind map to quickly capture that comparison.

If you hear words like "opinion," "view," or "side," then you're being told that what is being offered is subjective, so note it accordingly. Notice how the lecturer uses hypothetical questions, and how they are answering these questions. They are likely trying to indicate an underlying structure or argument. Similarly, if the lecturer says phrases like, "So where does that leave us?" or "In sum," or "Let's wrap up," for example, you know they are attempting to summarize or conclude, and you're being shown the outcome of the argument they have sketched for you thus far.

**Use discourse markers to guide your notes**

Your notes will essentially be a paraphrased version of the lecture you have heard. Paraphrasing is repeating the message of the lecture to yourself but in your own words, and its power lies in the fact that you don't merely parrot the same verbal data, but instead show your comprehension by expressing the deeper message of the lecture as a whole.

Verbatim note taking should be avoided, unless you're noting concrete factual details like names or dates. Your lecturer might say, "On the other hand, many people consider that the Jacquard loom was not a predecessor to the modern computer, but a full computer in its own right." You can note down: "Counterpoint: J loom = true computer." In one short sentence fragment, you have not only captured this detail, but you've also *processed* it in an active and attentive way, and you've paraphrased the key details.

Periodically review your notes–even directly after the lecture if possible–and tidy them up, making sure that everything is legible and that you haven't missed anything. "Translate" the notes into your own language and make them your own.

Active listening will produce notes that have richness and depth. When you revisit these notes, they will inspire a fuller engagement, and should you choose to revise from these notes or even use them to plan an essay, the quality of that work will be superior because it will be based on genuine understanding, and not mere rote and repetition.

## **Top-down Self-questioning for Deeper Comprehension**

Whether you are taking in new information by reading or by listening, the art of self-questioning can help you cultivate superior comprehension. **Learning to ask yourself questions before, during, and after engaging with new ideas keeps you active and focused**. The idea is not just to attend to the new information, but to monitor *yourself* through the learning process, continually asking how well you are comprehending what you read or hear.

This is why self-questioning (SQ) is called a top-down approach; you ask and answer your own questions while reading or listening. This empowers you to take responsibility for your learning process and reminds you of your agency in creating meaning from the new things you encounter. Bottom-up approaches, on the other hand, are limited to questions that passively come from the text or the lecturer. It might not always feel like it, but all of us are all capable of independently working our way through challenging concepts, and we don't have to rely on a text or a teacher to facilitate this process *for* us.

If you struggle to take in new information, don't be discouraged. Self-questioning techniques enable you to persevere on your learning journey, even if your materials are lacking or if your lecturer is not the best at explaining things. *You* can always be your own tutor, and strategic self-questioning is a great way to do this.

There is plenty of solid research suggesting that SQ is excellent for improving comprehension (National Reading Panel report, 2000; Sencibaugh, 2007; Nolan, 1991; Daniel & Williams, 2019) and that "Combining self-questioning strategy with paragraph restatement/summarization, main idea generation, and text structure analysis have yielded positive outcomes" (Willingham, 2006; 2007). Let's take a closer look at these strategies and how you can apply them yourself:

### Before: Preview and predict

You don't have to wait passively–prepare yourself in advance with questions which will prime you to recognize and absorb important information. Before entering a lecture or opening a book or article, ask questions like:

- Is this something you need to hear/read? Why?
- What is the overall topic or theme here?
- How does this topic or theme fit into your short- and long-term goals?
- Have you encountered anything like this before? If so, how does it connect here?

- What do you already know?
- What are your knowledge gaps in this area?
- After reading/listening, what do you hope to understand better?
- What do you predict this will be about?
- What questions do you already have?

**During: Evaluate and connect**

Once you are more fully engaged in the material, don't be tempted to drop back into a passive role, but instead continue to ask questions. These questions can certainly be about the material itself, but the real magic of SQ lies in questioning your own comprehension, blind spots, and overall response to the information you're taking in:

- Why is the author/speaker sharing this, in this way, at this time?
- How does all this connect to what I already know?
- How accurate were my predictions? What did I not anticipate?
- What am I struggling to see?
- What is the big idea here?

- What do I make of all this? What is my opinion or perspective?
- How can I actually use and apply what I'm encountering here?
- What is the most important takeaway for my own purposes?

**After: Summarize and reflect**

Just because the lecture is over or you're finished reading, doesn't mean you're finished engaging with the content! Keep asking questions:

- What do you now know that you didn't know before?
- Can you paraphrase and summarize the main message?
- Is there still something you don't understand?
- What could you do now to fill in the gaps– ask a question, seek help, read further?
- Have you been able to correct or fill in any gaps?
- What can you do now, given what you've learned?
- How effective was your note taking strategy?

- On reviewing your notes, what did you discover?
- Based on what you've read/heard, how might you like to approach the next text or lecture?

Self-questioning is a fantastic way to deepen your learning, develop transferable metacognitive skills, and build greater self-awareness. However, questions are always the start of something–never the end. Use your questions as tools to direct and support your own learning, rather than merely asking them and moving on.

Constantly be in the habit of interrogating not just the material in front of you, but the process you're in, and the quality of your own engagement. Challenge yourself to paraphrase and summarize everything that comes your way. Always be alert for the main idea, and for the underlying structure to which it is connected. Think in hierarchical levels, and be ready to zoom in and out accordingly, analyzing both the small and the large structure.

Finally, be your own teacher, and keep asking yourself questions. If you're confused, ask yourself what is confusing you, and why, and how you've found clarity in the past. If something is working well, ask yourself why, and how you can do more of it. If you can look back at your question driven notes, you will see a record of your learning journey over time. Through questions, not only are you learning about the material in question, but you are learning how to learn.

## Reverse outlining for better reading comprehension

A "reverse outline" is exactly what it sounds like. If an outline is a brief summary that we make in preparation to create a text, then **a reverse outline is a brief summary that we make of a text that already exists.** A reverse outline is not simply a summary, but resembles in every way the kind of outline we'd make for ourselves if we were the ones writing the text from scratch. By creating this outline, we gain more clarity on the key themes and ideas of that text, and how they're organized.

Making a reverse outline sounds simple, but in practice it takes care and attention–especially for more complex texts that you don't yet perfectly understand. Here are some steps to keep you focused:

**Step 1: Prepare and gather key information**

Start by reading the article twice. On your first read, just focus on understanding the general message and flow of the text. For example, while reading an article on climate change, you might notice that the emphasis seems to be specifically on how industrial practices impact the environment.

On the second read, write down keywords or ideas in the margins, such as "carbon footprint" or "sustainability." These are terms that answer the question, "What is this paragraph or section broadly about?"

You should ultimately have a list of relevant vocabulary words (find clear definitions using a dictionary, writing the definitions out if necessary). You are beginning to get a clear idea of the various components/elements making up this text, i.e., the overall content.

## Step 2: Organize your thoughts into an outline

In a notebook or word processor, begin to write down these main ideas in a bullet point list. These main ideas will either be the vocabulary terms you identified earlier, or, more likely, they will be concepts and ideas expanding on these words. For example, one item on your list could be, "Modern day clothing manufacturing has a high carbon footprint." For now, just list these ideas and themes in the order you find them in the text, and don't worry about full sentences. Your notes are essentially the answer to the question, "What is the specific claim that this paragraph or section is making?"

## Step 3: Refine and format your outline

By moving through steps 1 and 2, you are gradually reverse engineering an outline while identifying your text's main ideas and supporting ideas. The only thing to do now is to identify the conclusion of the whole piece.

Try to summarize and paraphrase the concluding remarks of your text, for example, "For climate change to be successfully addressed, changes need to be made to the biggest contributors, like industry."

Now you can format your outline properly. You can use the following structure:

**Thesis Statement:** Put this at the top of the page, for example: "Unsustainable industrial practices have one of the highest global carbon footprints, and so should be a priority when tackling climate change."

**Topic Sentence:** Write down a full sentence for each paragraph or sentence that neatly summarizes the main idea. The topic sentence of one paragraph, for example, might be: "The manufacture of cheap clothing and textiles is a particularly unsustainable industry." You may have similar sentences for several other components, let's say for the manufacture of plastics of electronics. Each of these is an example of "Unsustainable industry practices," which is the central theme.

**Evidence / Support:** Note down any evidence given for each of the main claims. Are there any statistics, graphs, studies? There may be real-life examples or even an argument made purely on logical grounds. In our example, one such piece of evidence may be a line from a cited journal article: "The fashion industry ranks as one of the most polluting industries, responsible for 10% of all carbon emissions and about 20% of global wastewater (Filho et. al., 2024)."

**Conclusion:** Note down the conclusion you found–although be aware that the conclusion might not be at the end. This is especially true with academic articles and papers, where the entire structure of the paper, conclusion included, will be at the top, in the abstract. Conclusions are often closely related to thesis statements. In our example, the conclusion might be: "New evidence strongly suggests that unsustainable industrial practices have one of the highest global carbon footprints, and so should be a priority when tackling climate change."

If you've followed this process carefully, what you should be left with is something nearly identical to the outline the author themselves used to write the piece. If you're feeling productive, you can even summarize this outline further into a simple single-paragraph.

The climate change example we've given here has been purposefully over-simplified, but in real life, certain texts can be truly baffling in their complexity. The reverse outlining technique helps you carefully reconstruct the "skeleton" beneath all this complexity, and as a result, your comprehension will improve.

Often, problems with reading comprehension happen because we are confused and distracted by the volume and complexity of the information we're seeing. We can't see how everything connects, why it's included, and what the point is. However, if we can first clarify the *implicit order* in a text, it suddenly becomes much easier to process the details.

**A few notes:**

- The author might not actually have the best rhetorical organization, and, if used as an evaluative tool, reverse outlining can be a powerful way to spot fallacious or weak arguments.
- There may not be one idea per paragraph, and the topic sentence will not necessarily be the first, or even clearly laid out as a single sentence at all.

- In real life articles and texts, it may be a little difficult to discern the difference between an example, an explanation, an opinion, a thesis statement etc., and there may be several weak lines of argument–or sometimes no argument at all!
- Finally, one productive way to extend this exercise is to challenge yourself to rewrite any texts that you find lacking in structure. Ask yourself what is missing, and what you would add to improve it.

No matter how complicated the text might have seemed at first, engaging with it to this depth will leave you feeling completely familiar and confident with the material, and you are not likely to forget what you've read (as a nice side-effect, reverse outlining will probably make you a better writer, too!).

**Summary:**

- Highlighting texts will only improve your comprehension when combined with more active, engaged study techniques. Most effective are the brain-book-buddy approach to draw attention to knowledge gaps, creative annotations that code

additional rich information, and self-generated questions for deeper understanding.
- Active listening requires full presence and mental engagement, and leads to notes that are more useful, especially for review. Create an environment conducive to listening, pay attention to discourse markers, and use the structure those discourse markers indicate to shape your own notes. Paraphrasing is an ideal way of interacting with and processing incoming information.
- Whether reading or listening to live lectures, self-questioning before, during, and after will keep you actively engaged, and help you monitor and interrogate your own learning process. You can practice SQ by first previewing and predicting, then connecting and evaluating ideas as you go, then finally by summarizing and reflecting.
- A reverse outline is a brief summary of a text that already exists; creating one can improve comprehension, especially of a text's deeper structure. Working backwards, gather key information,

organize it carefully, and shape it into an outline.

# Chapter Four: Deeper Comprehension and Lasting Memory

In this chapter, we will be building on the foundations of strong reading comprehension laid in the previous chapter. Engagement with a text falls on a continuum. At one end is the mere perception of new words, and the ability to read them and recognize the basic concept they're pointing to. But as we keep engaging further and further with what we read, we bring increasing amounts of our own intelligence to the meaning in the words, until we arrive at the other end of the continuum, where we have so deeply grasped and internalized that concept that it becomes a permanent part of our memory bank.

This chapter is all about the magic of building new knowledge onto old knowledge, of observation, of "overlearning," and of interacting with new material *physically*, that is, by writing things out by hand.

## **Writing by Hand Increases Memory**

With the increasing dependence on devices in every area of our lives, this question is more pressing than ever: is it better to write notes by hand, than to type them on a screen, such as in a word processor? The answer is: Yes and no. Digital note taking may certainly be more efficient, faster, and convenient. But if we use a different metric–i.e., the cognitive benefits–then digital note taking is significantly inferior to writing out notes in the old-fashioned way.

Research has consistently shown that writing notes out by hand brings distinct benefits for the learning process and can drastically improve learning and memory retention (Mueller & Oppenheimer, 2014). The reason for these findings is probably clear to you by now: active engagement. Ironically, it might be digital note taking's very speed and efficiency that makes it *worse* for comprehension and memory. Quickly typing something is just that–hitting keys on a keyboard. And then it's gone.

Taking the time to write something by hand, however, is a qualitatively different experience. You are more engaged. You are participating. When you write, you are *doing* something. You slow down, and you "explain" the concept to yourself and to the page, as it were. You are inviting your brain to take part in a process that simply does not happen to the same degree with digital notes.

Consider that humanity has been making marks on pages for thousands of years, but widespread at-home computer use has only been around for about 40 years. There is something in us that perceives a tangible, hand-written note as more permanent, more real, and, as it happens, more "noteworthy."

In contrast, for decades images on screens have been psychologically experienced as fleeting and impermanent, and associated with transience and entertainment. Evidence of the bias for the handwritten word is everywhere: People choose to record life's most important information in actual books or documents, and we are likely to be more trusting of a person's word when we can see their physical signature, written in their own hand, with real pen and ink.

All of this is to say that there is complicated and special relationship between the human brain and the physically written word–a relationship that cannot easily be replicated digitally. When we engage with new material, i.e., when we attempt to learn, the act of writing things by hand activates our brain's memory-making mechanisms. The more we engage when making the notes, the greater our later retention.

Human beings are visual, embodied, experiential learners. The way you process information is unique. It's said, "Tell me and I forget. Teach me and I remember. Involve me and I learn." Well, writing by hand is a way to involve yourself more deeply. When you write, you are triggering your brain's deep memories around the spatial properties of the letters you learnt as a toddler. The paper itself has a fixed size and location, it is here and now, and when you engage with it, your attention too is drawn more concretely into the present.

A 2021 Japanese study published in *Frontiers in Behavioral Neuroscience* found that writing by hand improved coding performance and was actually associated with greater neural activity in the areas of the brain connected with processing the location of information. Another study compared people's memory after being asked to schedule certain tasks, either on a tablet, a smartphone, or with pen and notebook. This latter group performed better in subsequent memory tests, and MRI scans showed greater brain responsiveness when they later performed the scheduled task (Umejima et. al., 2021). Another surprising finding was that taking notes by hand was actually faster, too.

Some studies have shown that typing instead of handwriting may actually damage children's early literacy skills (Dinehart, 2014, MacKenzie, 2019). This is because handwriting is about so much more than mere data capture; it is a multisensory skill we develop alongside our ability to think, process, and connect with the world around us, and convert it into symbols that we can remember, analyze, and manipulate mentally. Replacing all this with a simple press of a key on a keyboard bypasses all this additional complexity reducing meaning and memory to a fleeting digital flash, here one moment and gone the next.

The value of handwriting, then, is not just in the finished work we produce, but rather the process we take part in to produce that finished work. Here are a few practical ways you can use the process of handwriting to improve your memory retention:

**Paraphrase key ideas**

When taking notes by hand, try to avoid simply *copying* what you hear or read. If you can rewrite concepts in your own words, you immediately invite your brain to interact with those ideas, not just passively receive them.

**Pay attention to the tactile and the physical**

Handwriting is not a digital activity, but a physical act. Use notebooks, pens, and paper that you enjoy using, and keep your materials well-organized and cared for. Keep your notebooks in a prominent place in your study, or beside your bed. Choose colors, notebook designs, and paper that appeal to you aesthetically. The idea is not just to create more visual interest, but to activate as many parts of your brain as possible.

The physical act of writing itself can be a meditative practice, and a way to harness and focus your attention. Slow down and find stillness in the moment; form the letters mindfully, thinking about the deep connection between the symbol on the page, the concept you are trying to capture, and your intention to recall and understand it.

**Use different physical layouts for different topics**

Experiment with various note taking layouts to take full advantage of spatial cues. For example, create timelines for historical events, flowcharts for processes, or mind maps to capture certain relationships and hierarchies. Connecting text with other visual elements creates richer visual stimuli that will not only be easier to understand, but also easier to recall.

**Test your recall within 10 minutes of writing**

After taking notes, a good idea is to close your notebook and write down everything you can remember, without checking your notes. This exercise not only strengthens long-term memory by forcing your brain to retrieve fresh information, it also gives you an opportunity to rehearse the act of *graphically* reproducing memorized material. If you're studying for an exam, you will certainly improve retention and recall by closing the book and trying to recall certain details; however, if you make yourself write down these details, you are actually practicing the skill you will need in the exam itself.

## **Schema Activation in Reading Comprehension**

What *is* reading? One possible definition is that it is the process of discerning new meaning in a text, using prior meanings. A sentence may contain completely new information for us, yet we already know what each of the individual words mean and have encountered them before. By reading, we learn.

But what is learning? This is the process whereby we create a bridge between the knowledge we already possess, and new knowledge that we encounter.

Russell David from the wonderful teaching blog islandteacher.xyz says it perfectly:

> *"Reading comprehension is defined as the process of simultaneously extracting and constructing meaning through interaction and involvement with written language. Those involved in working with learners will know that meaning is not just derived from the learner's exposure to the text. What the reader brings to the text is hugely significant. These aspects include all the capacities, abilities, knowledge, and experiences that the person brings to the act of reading. These abilities enable the reader to unlock meaning."*

**Our prior "capacities, abilities, knowledge, and experiences" that we bring to learning a new text can be called schemata (plural of schema).** The term was originally coined as a psychological one; British psychologist Frederic Bartlett defined a schema as "an active organization of past reactions or experiences" (Shuying, 2013), but the word was soon used to describe the way background knowledge shapes a person's ability to comprehend new information. When we are trying to comprehend something we don't know, all we have to use are things that we *do* know.

**Making sense of texts**

To improve our reading comprehension, we need to get better at identifying and digesting the meaning inside texts. You might know perfectly well how to read, but unless you can grasp the *meaning* in those words, you are not really reading at all. Schemata help us do this; mastering reading comprehension therefore means mastering the use of our schemata.

Schemata are always changing, and good readers know how to activate the right ones before, during, and after every text they encounter. This is precisely what we have been attempting to do with the various techniques covered in this book, including self-questioning, reverse outlining, and, in particular, the ADEPT method, which we'll discuss in the next chapter.

The academic theory behind schema activation can be complex, but for our purposes, the idea is simple: **we learn by making connections, and drawing meaningful links between new ideas and the things we already know.** If we can consciously draw on the frameworks and connections our brain is already making, we can learn more quickly and more effectively. This applies to *all* learning, not just the learning we do by reading.

**Before you read,** prepare yourself by thinking about everything you already know about the topic to come.

**While you read,** actively look for new connections between ideas, and be ready to adjust and tweak existing schemata so they grow and change as your understanding improves.

**After you read,** consolidate all this new growth and change to your schemata by reflecting, taking notes, discussing your insights, or applying the lessons in some way. The real magic happens when your new, updated schema is carried to your next text/lesson.

What schema activation looks like

**Connect Text to Personal Experiences**

*Question to ask: "How does this relate to my life?"*

It's about connections, and one important connection to make is the one between yourself and the text you're reading. You are a unique human being, and your response to a text will be your own. How does what you're reading connect to your own history, experiences, memories, and knowledge? This goes beyond merely deciding whether you agree or not; rather, try to *personalize* your understanding of this text. Find a link between its style, content, or structure.

The idea is to activate a kind of introspection within you that will enhance your own understanding and memory.

**Contextualize**

*Question to ask: "How does this relate to the world?"*

The next connection to make is the one between the text and its broader context, i.e., the world that it exists in. There will be a relationship there–is it a contentious one? An old one? A confusing one? Become curious not just about the themes and ideas being covered, but how the text itself is treating those themes, and how that treatment is a reflection of the time, place, and cultural context that produced that text.

You might ask who the author is, where they're from, and what school of thought or movement they belong to. What is the text an expression of? How does it relate to bigger sociopolitical or economic events currently unfolding?

**Identify Similarities Across Works**

*Question to ask: "How does this connect to other texts?"*

Nothing exists in a vacuum. All written works are, in a way, smaller parts of a larger conversation that unfolds across many different works and authors, over time. Become curious about where the text you're currently reading fits into this broader scheme. In what ways is it similar to other works you've already read or heard about? In what ways is it different?

As you look for intertextual patterns and relationships, your comprehension of all of them will deepen. Incidentally, this is precisely the kind of reading that the Zettelkasten method is designed to support. As you read, you might think, "What does this remind me of?" and that may trigger you to create the notes that will gradually grow your own "personal wiki."

In this way, you can carefully elaborate on and extend your existing sum of knowledge, scaffolding new layers and levels with every new lesson. If we can consciously connect the old to the new in this way, we not only improve comprehension, but memory. It's much easier to recall newly learned material if it is connected to older, more established knowledge: we recall the old, and the new comes along with it.

### **The Art of Observational Note Taking**

We have spoken about note taking during live lectures, and of note taking during reading.

But there is another way to use strategic note taking, and that is to assist the observation of more natural, "real-life" scenarios and situations. Knowing how to record and analyze the notes we take about real life phenomena is a rich, but often underappreciated skill. The following techniques are about the practical learning that comes about from closely watching living systems in real-time, rather than simply reading or hearing about those systems.

When might observation of this kind be useful? Examples include:

- Market research–how are customers behaving in their natural environment?
- Competitor analysis
- Scientific and ethnographic research
- Troubleshooting issues with dynamic systems, such as an organization or business
- Creative and open-ended observation, i.e., people-watching or artistic life study
- The development of school curricula
- Conflict resolution or mediation

The AEIOU Framework

**The AEIOU Framework is heuristic framework that provides an intelligent approach to organizing and structuring any act of observation.** The framework comes from the world of UX design and the development of digital products and software, and was originally created by Rick E Robinson as a way to structure a "contextual inquiry." In other words, the acronym is most often used to help organize research into software product design and usability.

However, don't let this fool you; the AEIOU approach is an intelligent way to structure *any* act of observation, and can be very successfully combined with any of the other note taking approaches in this book.

AEIOU stands for the following 5 heuristic categories:

Activities

Environments

Interactions

Objects

Users

Each category is something that a researcher (in this case, you) might observe and document "in the field." It's essentially a method of structuring the way you capture data as it unfolds.

- **Activities:** What are people actually doing? Take note of the behaviors that people do to achieve their goals.

- **Environments:** Where is all this happening? Take note of the overall setting of the behavior.

- **Interactions:** If there is more than one person, how are they relating to one another? How are these people in turn relating to the environment? What effect is the environment having on them, and what effect are they having on the environment?

- **Objects:** What are the specific objects in the environment? How are these specific objects connecting to people, to people's behaviors? How are the objects mediating or influencing the interactions?

- **Users:** Who exactly are you observing? What are their personalities, perspectives, and priorities? What are their goals and how are they engaging with other elements in the environment to achieve those goals?

Granted, all of this may seem rather abstract and high-level, but this is precisely what makes this framework so useful for so many different observation tasks. Knowing how to pay close attention to our surroundings can yield incredible insights that are simply not available to us just by reading or listening. No matter what you are studying or investigating, strategic observation will help you "read" and "listen" to the world around you in an expanded way. Just like the other methods we've discussed, this one brings clarity in that it encourages us to break concepts down and investigate the relationships between those concepts.

To put the AEIOU acronym to use, simply take a worksheet like the one below into "the field"–whatever that is for you–and gather observational data, step by step. Make sure you have clarified your research goal first, and if possible, write that at the top of the page.

| Activities | Environments | Interactions | Objects | Users |
|---|---|---|---|---|
|  |  |  |  |  |

DATE: | PROJECT NAME: | TYPE OF RESEARCH:
TIME: | RESEARCHER NAME:

From *Open Practice Library*, Darcie Fitzpatrick, accessed 2025 https://openpracticelibrary.com/practice/aeiou-observation-framework/

Before we consider how this framework might be put into practice, let's consider a closely related heuristic framework, captured by the acronym POEMS.

The POEMS Framework

POEMS stands for:

People

Objects

Environments

Messages

Services

This is more suitable for investigating communication or the use of tools in a system, i.e., understanding how messages and services are reciprocally influencing the behavior of people and objects in an environment. This acronym may be better suited to systems where the communication of a message is crucial, or a service is being somehow delivered. Such systems might be found in educational contexts, social media marketing, governmental services, broadcasting, or even public health. Below is a possible template you could use:

From *Atomicobject.com*, Kimberly Crawford, 2024, accessed 2025

https://spin.atomicobject.com/wp-content/uploads/20170915111358/POEMS Template.pdf

Applying AEIOU and POEMS in Observational Note Taking

Let's put some of these tools to use.

### Step 1: Identify subjects and location

The first step in your observational exercise is to identify who or what you're observing, and the location you're observing them in. This could be an individual, a group of people, or even an object, and the setting could be a public or private space, or even a natural environment.

Software and UX designers, for example, want to better understand how real people actually live, what their lives are like, what jobs they're doing, and what the current processes in question look like. So, before they even create a new piece of software, they go and observe their potential customers and users dealing with the problem that they hope the new software will solve.

**Step 2: Prepare a worksheet**

Use either the POEMS or AEIOU worksheets above, or devise your own version. Print it out, ensuring that there is enough space for you to take your notes. If you anticipate making lots of observations, you may wish to print out several sheets, or else dedicate a full page to a single category. Also jot down date, time, and location, as well as any details about your overall goals.

**Step 3: Conduct your observation**

Now it's time to start observing. Quietly take note of everything happening around you.

Note what is happening, to whom, and why. This may take concerted focus and attention on your part.

For AEIOU, observe the actions people are engaged in (Activities), the layout and setting of the place (Environments), how people interact with each other and their surroundings (Interactions), the objects they're using (Objects), and the people involved (Users).

For POEMS, track who is involved (People), the items or tools they are interacting with (Objects), the setting (Environments), the messages being exchanged (Messages), and the systems or services they are using (Services).

The length of your observation will depend on you and your goals, but a minimum of an hour is typically recommended. You'll know that you've gathered enough data when it seems as though new observations are simply covering old ground, rather than adding anything new.

In our software example, the designers might observe over the course of an hour how people are struggling to perform a particular task with their current IT system and note all the temporary solutions users devise over the course of their workday. They might observe how certain parts of the environment frequently impeded their efforts, but that the work team itself cooperates and quickly shares information verbally, even when the IT systems fail. The observer notes all this without comment or judgment.

**Step 4: Review**

When you're done, go through each category and see what you can make of the data. Look for themes, see what questions or answers you have generated, link ideas, or devise a plan given your new insights. Of course, the way you review will depend on the research question or goal you started with. If you were a software designer, for example, and your question was broadly, "Do people really need this new thing I want to develop?" you might analyze your observations and try to see what demand you could reasonably expect.

Don't worry if you can't find a natural way to make this form of observational note taking work for you. However, don't assume that observation plays no role at all in your note taking work–intelligent observation is the very foundation of good note taking. It can be incredibly illuminating to occasionally pause and observe yourself and your own environment in real time. By applying strategic observation to our own learning processes, we can diagnose problems, spot hidden solutions and opportunities, and develop more self-awareness. Being more aware of objects, messages, people, environments, and the interactions between them allows you to better comprehend not particular phenomenon, but entire ecosystems.

## **Overlearning for Subject Mastery**

The principle of overlearning is captured in the quote: "An amateur practices until they can do something correctly; a professional practices until they can't do something incorrectly."

Many people use notes, study tools, and materials in an entirely temporary way–they learn just enough to get them through the test, the game, or the recital, but no more. Once they "get it," they stop. This may be fine if a particular goal is not all that important, but if you're interested in deeper, more lasting learning, then you need to go a little further.

Learning just enough to get the job done teaches you just that–how to get the job done. For deeper mastery you need repetition and further study, i.e., overlearning.

A fascinating study titled "Overlearning Hyperstabilizes a Skill by Rapidly Making Neurochemical Processing Inhibitory-dominant" (Shibata et. al., 2017) defines overlearning as **"the continued training of a skill after performance improvement has plateaued."**

The authors' findings were most interesting:

> "...overlearning in humans abruptly changes neurochemical processing, to hyperstabilize and protect trained perceptual learning from subsequent new learning. Usually, learning immediately after training is so unstable that it can be disrupted by subsequent new learning until after passive stabilization occurs hours later. However, **overlearning so rapidly and**

**strongly stabilizes the learning state that it not only becomes resilient against, but also disrupts, subsequent new learning."**

Such a phenomenon was called "hyperstabilization" by the authors. After we learn something new, we can be said to possess new knowledge and skills, but this is still a tenuous gain. We can still forget, fall into old habits, or lose that mastery. With overlearning, we cement our learning so that it's not just something we can do well, but something we couldn't do poorly if we tried.

While there is value in challenging yourself to grow by increasing difficulty, overlearning is a strategy for reinforcing and internalizing material that we don't ever want to forget. If we apply this to note taking for learning purposes, we can see that repetition and repeated review of notes can lead to the hyperstabilization mentioned above. After sufficient overlearning, it would take more effort to try and forget these things than it takes to recall them.

Locking in Knowledge and Skill

To overlearn, all we need to do is continue to rehearse, practice, or review despite our proficiency. Because we continue on at the same level of difficulty, overlearning can never lead to more learning, but it can *reinforce* learning. This may feel a little counterintuitive at first, and even boring, but drilling skills and knowledge this way definitely has its advantages.

Examples of where you might want to "lock in" what you learn:

- Sports like basketball or golf, where accuracy of a single repeated move is critical. By rehearsing the correct sequence over and over, sportsmen can develop an almost permanent "muscle memory" so that they could hit the bull's eye almost in their sleep.
- Public performances like speeches, standup, music, dance, or acting, where the precise delivery of lines, moves, or musical notes becomes so deeply embedded that they can be done effortlessly and naturally.

- Mathematics, chess, or coding, where certain individuals have memorized certain equations of operations and can draw on them quickly and easily as they solve more complex problems.

In fact, overlearning may be a big part of why some people can go so far in their chosen fields; they rehearse and internalize certain basic components of their field to such an extent that it no longer takes any cognitive effort. Onto this scaffold, they can then build more challenging, more complex skills. It's a little similar to how, if you could learn to ride a unicycle without even thinking about it, you could more easily learn to juggle while doing it.

A study published in the *Journal of Neuroscience* bears this out: The researchers found that as study participants got better and better at a certain motor skill, their muscle activity declined–this is expected since the body is becoming more efficient at the task (Huang et. al., 2012). Learning to ride a unicycle is incredibly taxing and difficult at first, but as you learn, you get better, and you spend less energy trying to stay upright.

The truly fascinating thing, however, was that the participants' energy usage continued to decline, until the participants themselves reported feeling that the task wasn't even happening anymore. This is like riding a unicycle flawlessly, without even thinking about it.

"The message from this study," says Alaa Ahmed, the lead researcher, "is that, in order to perform with less effort, keep on practicing, even after it seems the task has been learned [...] there is an advantage to continued practice beyond any visible changes in performance."

When you overlearn something, it becomes second nature, and impossible to forget.

**Tip 1: Go beyond proficient**

Once you've understood a topic or solved a problem correctly, continue practicing. Keep drilling the skill or reviewing the information. It may feel boring at times or as though nothing is happening, but each repetition is cementing the concept deeper into your mind by tiny degrees.

**Tip 2: Use spaced repetition**

Overlearning is so effective that it can actually interfere with the retention and stability of tasks you undertake afterwards–for up to four hours later. Try to avoid scheduling new learning tasks directly after an overlearning session. It's a great idea to leave overlearning as the last activity for the day; a good night's sleep will help your brain further consolidate and cement your overlearning efforts.

### Tip 3: Simulate exam conditions

After overlearning a topic, test yourself in a setting that mimics the pressures of a real exam. For example, practice timed quizzes or present your answers to a classmate to simulate performing under scrutiny. This helps prepare you for the actual test environment, ensuring you can recall the information and apply it under pressure. The more realistic the practice, the more confident you'll feel on test day.

### Tip 4: Be mindful

Overlearning should not be used as a way to avoid or procrastinate doing more challenging work, and you should take care that you are not overlearning very basic tasks to give you a false sense of competence. It's important to carefully consider which tasks are best approached with overlearning, and which aren't. Overlearning is not suitable for every task and may devolve into mindless rote practice if done incorrectly.

Save overlearning for repeatedly used, foundational components of larger and more complex tasks, and mentally rehearse these things only after you've spent time challenging yourself to cover new material. For example, you might spend all morning creating new notes for fresh material from class lectures, but on your way home in the late afternoon, you close your eyes on the train and mentally rehearse the basics again and again.

**Summary:**

- Writing notes by hand may be more inefficient in some ways, but usually leads to better memory and comprehension because it provides more active cognitive engagement. Humans are visual, tactile, and experiential learners who learn best through the physical process of handwriting.

- Schemata are our prior capacities, abilities, knowledge, and experiences that, when strategically activated, give us access to new concepts. We learn by making connections and drawing meaningful links between new ideas and the things we already know.
- AEIOU and POEMS are two heuristic frameworks designed to organize observational learning. These note taking methods allow us to conduct contextual investigations and "read" systems in real-time. Decide on your observation goal, print out a worksheet, and then make careful observations which you can later review and act on.
- Overlearning means continuing to practice even after we have "got it." Repetition and continuous review of notes leads to *hyperstabilization*. With mindful use of overlearning strategies, we deeply internalize information and can never forget it.

# Chapter Five: Master Abstraction, Analysis, and Critical Thinking

Let's move a little further along that continuum we spoke about earlier. We have been exploring in some detail how to read books or articles, but how do we select what to read and what to ignore? How can we evaluate and appraise the things we've comprehended, once we've figured out how to comprehend them? And what should we do about texts that are really difficult or unfamiliar?

In this chapter, our focus will be on all those note taking methods that rely on higher-order skills such as abstraction, analysis, and critical thinking. We are gradually widening our field of awareness to include information **well beyond the text itself**, learning to think contextually, and with discernment.

## Reading Analytically Through Pigeonholing

Every instance of learning is, by definition, an encounter with something initially unknown to us. By its very nature, the act of learning means approaching the unknown and asking it, "What is this?"

However, this question can be asked and answered on many different levels. If I have never seen sheet music in my life, I can become curious and try to learn about it. What is this? Clearly, the marks on the page mean something. Slowly, I could learn that this is a kind of language, and I could figure out the rules of that language. In a sense, this would be answering my initial question.

But sheet music is made for a purpose–to guide the actions of a musician as they make music. If I mistakenly treat the musical notation on the page as nothing more than a kind of code, I know much about it, but I haven't really answered the question.

When we develop our faculties for deeper, analytical thinking about the various unknowns in front of us, we pay attention to the higher-order *function* and *purpose* of not just the phenomenon in question, but particular information about the phenomenon. If we understand the purpose of sheet music, for instance, or the purpose of music more generally, then we understand on a deeper level what it *is*.

To fine-tune our own analytical understanding of the things we're learning about, we need to master **pigeonholing, which is the art of identifying something's function and purpose before we engage with it.** The concept was first popularized by the Adler and Doren's 1940 classic *How to Read a Book* (highly recommended, by the way). By pigeonholing, we prepare ourselves to interact with information in the right way. Because we know what *kind* of thing it is, we can ask the right questions, and structure our learning accordingly.

Thinking that musical notation is a kind of code completely misses its real function, no matter how clever you are at breaking that code. Unless you can understand the broader context in which sheet music exists, you haven't really comprehended it. No matter how hard you've worked to understand the notes on the page, until you've grasped what was happening *beyond* the page, you haven't really understood.

By pigeonholing, we correctly place a thing in the right context, and tailor our reading approach accordingly. Pigeonholing tends to refer to the intake of information from books, but it can be expanded to include any information type.

Even if we don't know much about the topic at hand, we can first identify the broad category it belongs to in order to meet the demands the book may make of us:

- Fiction such as novels and poetry ask that our engagement is more aesthetic, emotional, and thematic. We are invited to immerse ourselves in a world, not analyze it.
- Scientific arguments ask that we engage by following and appraising the logic and flow, evaluating the evidence.
- Philosophical works require that we engage on the systematic and abstract foundational level, beyond specific details.

- Instructions and technical textbooks ask us merely to comprehend and implement.
- Personal accounts, experimental works, and open-ended investigations ask to engage with curiosity and empathy, or merely to witness.

We might be exceptionally good at processing information details on one level, but if we have failed to properly classify a book, then we may find ourselves with serious misunderstandings. We might treat Darwin's *Origin of the Species* as a personal or historical treatise (when it is a formal scientific argument), or we might mistakenly start analyzing the logic and coherence of a work the author intended as an artistic expression. We might mistake plain instruction for an argument offered up for our consideration, or treat a serious philosophical work as a mere style piece or expression of personal taste. Worse still, we may mistake news for entertainment, or advertisements for public information.

Ultimately, misclassifying texts before we engage with them leads to plenty of confusion and invariably wastes our time. There are three straightforward steps we can rely on to pigeonhole a text properly and ensure that we're adopting a reading strategy that will do it justice.

**Step 1: Find the broad category**

Briefly, is the book fiction or non-fiction? This is usually the broadest and most definitive difference, and one that could prove disastrous if not properly clarified.

The distinction may seem simple enough in the above definitions, but many books straddle categories. Some works, for example, will initially look like factual historical accounts of events and time periods, but on closer inspection the work is fictional, and only *inspired* by history, either thematically or aesthetically. In a similar way, many pop-science books on the market today are not truly non-fiction, but are better approached as personal conjecture, despite appearances and marketing!

**Step 2: Find the purpose**

Texts are created for a *reason*, and this reason will inform the kind of reading you bring to it. A text can have one or more purposes:

- To persuade
- To inform
- To teach
- To entertain
- To inspire and encourage
- To deceive (unfortunately)
- Finally, to opine (expository works share theories, opinions, speculations, or hypotheses)

It's important that we don't confuse *our* purposes with the *author's* purposes.

We might sincerely adore Marcus Aurelius and other Stoic authors, and we may personally find plenty of wisdom and truth in their works, but if we are trying to compile a historically accurate account of everyday life in ancient Rome, these are not the ideal texts to turn to.

## Step 3: Adjust your reading style

Once you have clearly identified the kind of thing you are reading, and the reason it was written in the first place, then you are best primed to read accordingly. Refer back to the text's purpose.

- If it is to persuade: Carefully and fully evaluate the argument offered up, and evaluate and scrutinize its premises.
- If it is to inform or teach: Commence breaking down and organizing the data to understand and apply it.
- If it is to entertain, inspire, or encourage: No special intellectual effort is required! Engage your emotions, and receive the message with your higher sentiments and perceptions.
- If it is to deceive: Recognize the deception clearly and discount it.

The more difficult, information-heavy, or important a work, the slower you need to read. More lightweight entertainment can be taken in quickly, since you will not need to scrutinize the narrative, but merely experience and enjoy it.

To strengthen your own pigeonholing muscle, here are some texts to think about, and have fun classifying:

- Margaret Mitchell's *Gone with the Wind* (Epic novel? History book? "Chick lit"?)
- Shakespeare's *Romeo and Juliet* (Is it a play, or a book? Is it a serious treatise on human nature, or an entertaining teenage love story?)
- The Old Testament of the Bible (Historical account? Wisdom literature? Philosophical argument?)

If you find yourself unsure, zoom in on the author's most likely intention and purpose for the book. Even if you cannot accurately classify a book (a common issue when works are complex), you can still make efforts to match your style of reading to the intention with which it was written.

Scan the title and book description, or read summaries or introductory paragraphs. Consider the author, the date, and where the book is sold or made available. Finally, a few questions to make your pigeonholing more effective:

- Is this work theoretical or practical? (I.e., is it knowledge for its own sake or knowledge for utility's sake?)

- What is the main topic, and what is the perspective on that topic?
- Is there any moral, ethical, or ideological slant? Or is the material presented without judgment?
- Is the book itself asking a question, or making a statement? What is that statement–a complaint, a summary, an observation?

## **The Three Level Reading Guide–from Shallow to Deep**

Once you've identified the kind of book or article you're reading, and the kind of attention you should bring to it, then you're ready to begin reading in earnest. One way to structure and organize your reading is to think of it in terms of three levels:

1. The literal meaning–*on the lines*
2. The inferred meaning and interpretation–*between the lines*
3. The context and application–*beyond the lines*

To read well means to be cognizant of the many different layers of meaning in any text, and to comprehend the facts and details on the surface, the hidden meaning beneath the surface, and the meaning that might exist outside of the book altogether. Being able to shift from literal understanding to critical thinking is a skill essential to reading–and every other area of life that requires problem-solving, synthesis, or deep comprehension. Let's take a closer look at each level.

**Level 1: Reading "on the lines"**

This is, simply put, the level at which you understand the facts that are put in front of you. This is a straightforward question of the explicit and stated facts in the text, for example the name of a character, the exact event that unfolded, when, and where. We explored this level in our very first chapter.

To read at this level is to practice basic comprehension of the text as-is. As you read, note down or highlight key details, not unlike the way you identified the "5Ws and an H" in the GIST technique described earlier. Questions to ask: Who, what, when, where?

As an example, let's say you are reading a popular bestselling autobiography about a famous investor. It's a non-academic and non-technical book, but you're a beginner with this topic, and choose this book as a starting point to give you a feel for some of the key themes.

You read the first chapter and it's all about the famous investor's history, with specific details about types of investments, as well as a simple explanation of how the stock market works. As you read, you stop now and then to take notes. What is the author actually saying? You spend some time making sure you grasp the plain facts he's offering in black and white. Perhaps you do this by highlighting key details, jotting down bullet points, and making a quick summary.

**Level 2: Reading "between the lines"**

The next level is to consider what the explicitly expressed information from level 1 is really pointing to. What meanings can we *infer*, even though they are not stated outright? What are the broader themes that are developing, and how are events connecting to one another?

Questions to ask: Why? What does X mean? What are the consequences of Y? What is Z an example of, or what does it look like? What do

I predict will come next? What is the "bigger picture" here?

To return to our example, you also note that as you're reading this very straightforward and informative text, you can't help but wonder *why* the author is sharing all these details about his life, or why he's chosen these specific ones. Though the message is never laid out explicitly, it all leads to an unspoken proposition: If a person could emulate some of this man's characteristics or his approach to money, then they too might experience his success. Thus, certain details take on extra, hidden meanings; some anecdotes seem to serve as a warning, some as inspiration, some as encouragement... even though all this detail is strictly between the lines.

### Level 3: Reading "beyond the lines"

The book we're reading is actually part of a meta-text called *life*, and it connects meaningfully to this wider context. This level of reading is deep and broad: What other authors, arguments, themes, or stories connect to this one? How does this book fit into the bigger historical and cultural landscape? What's the context, and what role does this book play in that context?

When it comes to our own lives, we can carefully consider whether and to what extent we agree with what we've read, and how we might like to synthesize the overall message with everything else we know on this topic, and everything else we've read so far. Depending on the type of book, we might amend our opinion or decide to take a certain action based on what we've read. The more we can generalize and extrapolate a book into our world, the more we can gain from reading it.

Questions to ask: What do I think of X? What does this other person think of X? Where does this fit? How can I apply this? What bigger pattern is this book a part of? What is this book an example of? What does it connect to? What are the alternatives? What do I do now that I've read this book? What decisions, judgments, or new questions do I have?

To return to our example, you might finish the book and take some time to process what you've read. Do you agree with the implied worldview that went into the creation of this book? Do you believe that the account is actually true, or do you suspect that there might be some "spin"? What do you make of the fact that other celebrity investment gurus criticize the author? Do you agree with their criticism? What is the purpose of this book, and what exactly did the author hope to achieve with it? Given what you've read, are you going to make any changes to your life or to your money management strategy?

In many ways, it is only at the second and third level that our reading really comes alive; it is when we properly digest, process, analyze, and interpret the superficial facts of a text that we start to properly engage with it. That said, we cannot do this well unless we have an accurate foundation in the details and have read with clear and organized perception first.

Reading a work completely (that is, at every possible level) requires time and effort. Most importantly, it requires our active engagement. We need to dialogue with what we read, we need to take it apart, and we need to look at it through many different lenses of understanding. For important works that have the chance to actually change our lives, we need to go well beyond mere comprehension of data and move into real *participation*.

## **The SPE Method for Better Critical Reading**

Pigeonholing is not the only useful critical reading tool introduced in Adler and Doren's *How to Read a Book*. The SPE method is a great tool for analyzing a text's deeper underlying structure and message, particularly when reading more theoretical or philosophical non-fiction texts.

When you read a sentence, your brain is working hard to make sense of the grammar of that sentence, because the meaning the sentence points to is embedded within this structure. It's important, for example, to really understand the difference between "The dog bit the boy." and "The boy bit the dog." for example, because structure matters, and it helps reveal meaning.

**The SPE method (structure, propositions, and evaluate) is a way of grasping the proverbial "grammar" of a text, i.e., the structure that, if properly grasped, will reveal the text's meaning.** This is what makes SPE ideal for things like academic essays, philosophical arguments, articles, scientific papers, or persuasive pieces like speeches or treatises. These kinds of texts are, much like basic sentences, making claims and arguments. If we understand the structure and shape of these arguments, we are better able to understand what we're reading, as well as formulate a worthwhile response to it.

While we've already seen that misunderstandings can arise when we approach a textual argument without realizing that it is a textual argument (we pigeonhole it incorrectly) we also make an error when we fail to fully grasp what the argument is or when we find ourselves responding to claims that have not been made.

One massive misconception made by inexperienced readers is to think that their only job when reading a new piece of non-fiction is to decide whether they agree or not. They may be in such a hurry to make this evaluation that they scarcely take the time to clarify *what* it is they are agreeing or disagreeing with in the first place. The SPE method is a good corrective to this tendency, since it brings our attention to *structure* first, ensuring that we don't get distracted or misled by content or style. **Step 1: Identify the underlying structure**

Before you dive in to read, look at the way the text has been organized and laid out. Consider the table of contents, the titles and subtitles, the images, charts and tables, any supplementary material, etc.

It's crucial to understand that this literal layout of the printed words and images is *not* the structure we are looking to identify. Rather, this layout can give us hints about what the deeper structure and purpose of the text may be. In other words, it's not just about looking at the elements included, but at their order, and the implicit claims made by that ordering.

For example, there may be a book titled *The Case Against Social Media* and it may contain chapter titles such as, "What is Social Media?," "Taking Stock," and "The Evidence"–a chapter that contains graphs, charts, and other quantitative and statistical data. Chapters near the end include "Summing Up," and "Where to Now?"

Even though the book is not a true scientific report, this layout strongly suggests the shape of the argument being made: A hypothesis is posed, a study designed and conducted, results gathered, and a closing discussion is offered. At a glance, you can also see that the author will not be presenting a moral, sociological, or cultural discussion, and won't be sharing conjectures about the cause of the problem, nor their personal opinion on solutions. Instead, as suggested by their title, they are simply trying to convince you of the evidence against social media use.

## Step 2: Identify the argument's propositions

Every argument is made up of propositions, or premises. These are claims or assertions that, when strung together in a logical order, lead to the main point being made, i.e., the conclusion of the argument. We need only a basic understanding of logic to grasp the scaffolding of any argument:

- Premise 1
- Premise 2
- Conclusion

For example:

- A mammal is an animal that gives birth to live young
- Whales give birth to live young
- Therefore, a whale is a mammal

In the above argument, the premises are offered in a logical, meaningful sequence that supports the final conclusion.

- When it rains, the ground gets wet
- It is raining
- Therefore, the ground will get wet

At this stage, we are only identifying the premises and locating their position in the argument. It is not important yet what the premises are, only the role they play in the overall structure. There are broadly three kinds of argument:

1. Deductive (of which the above are examples): These arguments are "top down"; the premises lead directly to the conclusion.
2. Inductive: These arguments are "bottom up" or "reasoning from example".

3. Abductive: These arguments are collecting observations to support the conclusion.

We do not have the time nor space here to explore the entire realm of formal logic, but there are two vital skills you need at this point. You must be able to both discern the difference between premises and conclusions, and to understand the difference between identifying flaws in *content* and identifying flaws in *logical structure*.

Let's say the (very simplified) argument we find in *The Case Against Social Media* is essentially:

- Premise 1: Mental illness manifests in certain ways: XYZ
- Premise 2: Social media use manifests the identical attributes: XYZ
- Conclusion: Therefore, Social Media use creates mental illness

**Step 3: Carefully evaluate**

In this step, consider the truth of each of the premises and propositions made, and whether the conclusion logically follows from each of them. If a conclusion logically follows from its premises, the argument is considered *valid*. An argument is invalid if its conclusion is not supported by its premises in this way. Note that an argument can be valid even if the premises are untrue. If, however, the premises are true *and* the conclusion logically follows, the argument is considered *sound*.

Knowing this, reconsider the argument against social media above. Ask yourself whether the logic is valid, and whether the conclusion really does follow from the premises. Be careful with this–it's not always as obvious as you think. If you're having trouble sorting it out for yourself, take a look at the following simplified example:

- When it rains, the ground gets wet
- The ground is wet
- Therefore, it must be raining

Of course, you can imagine that the ground may be wet for some other reason, for example someone has spilled some water on it. The above argument is invalid and its conclusion unsupported, even though both its premises are true. Can you see how something similar might be happening in the social media argument?

This level of analysis may seem painstaking and tricky at first, but if you can see beyond the content of an argument to its structure, you drastically improve the quality of the information you take in, and learn to quickly discern between high quality arguments and those that are not worth your time and effort. You may be extremely masterful at processing information, but it won't be worth much if you can neither comprehend nor verify the underlying logical structure. Mastering this skill alone will grant you a degree of critical discernment that most readers do not possess.

## **ADEPT Method**

If you are truly challenging yourself to grow past your limits and expand your horizons, then you *will* find yourself frequently grappling with material that feels complicated, unfamiliar, and even a little overwhelming. This is never a sign that you are lacking in any way, but merely an indication that you are functioning at the vanguard of your understanding, and not within your cognitive comfort zone. To feel challenged in this way is a good thing!

That said, it's useful to have some strategies to help you grasp what might at first seem ungraspable. **Understanding what you don't yet understand requires a kind of conceptual leap; the ADEPT method is a collection of different ways we can make that leap.**

No matter how intimidating a new or difficult concept seems, you can always get on top of it by breaking it down, looking at it from a different perspective, or seeing what else it connects to in the world-especially to those things you *are* familiar with. The acronym stands for:

Analogy – "What is it like?"

Diagram – "How can I visualize it?"

Example – "How can I experience it for real?"

Plain English – "How can I put this in everyday language?"

Technical definition – "What exactly are the formal details?"

**Analogy**

It's a quirk of the human intellect that it can best grasp what a thing is by first understanding something that it isn't. Analogies are metaphors that point to relationships and connections. You understand one part of the analogy, but not the other. The analogy itself serves as a bridge, so that the new thing is now a little more comprehensible.

Let's consider a phenomenon in physics called the Doppler Effect. A good analogy might be the following: "The Doppler Effect is like tossing pebbles into a pond while running. If you're moving toward the water, the ripples bunch up closer together in front of you. If you're moving away, the ripples spread farther apart. This is similar to how sound waves behave when the source of the sound is moving."

Here, you start with something accessible, i.e., the behavior of ponds, water, and ripples, and connect it meaningfully to something not yet understood–the behavior of sound waves. Many scientific models and theories can be understood as expanded analogies and metaphors: The human eye works like a camera, an electron is like a ball, subatomic particles are like vibrating strings, etc.

Now, the two things being compared in an analogy don't have to be alike in every aspect–only in that aspect that you are trying to grasp and understand. It's just the finger pointing at the moon, not the moon itself (a famous recursive Buddhist analogy about the relationship between language and reality).

**Diagram**

Diagrams can help you access material in a deeper way than mere verbal explanation can. Use charts, symbolic depictions, illustrations, etc., to *visually* capture a concept or idea. Drawing diagrams in this way activates different parts of your brain and may allow for that crucial "Aha!" moment of comprehension.

In our example, you might need to visually see a diagram of a moving car with a horn emitting sound waves. In front of the car, the waves are closer together (high frequency), and behind the car, the waves are farther apart (low frequency).

**Example**

Abstract concepts can be difficult to grasp because we cannot experience them directly with our senses, and we don't have any real-life instances to look to as representatives of that concept. None of us can ever perceive with our sense organs an electron, a subatomic particle, or the complicated action of the human eye. You might be able to verbally and visually understand the Doppler Effect, but it may only be when you're literally observing it in real time that you fully grasp what it is. Indeed, many groundbreaking scientific experiments have their effect for this reason; they are able to make manifest to our sense organs the action of something ordinarily not available to our sense organs.

In our example, you can stand on the sidewalk and pay attention to the way that a passing ambulance siren's sound changes as it approaches you, then drives away. As it approaches, the siren sounds higher pitched. Once it passes and moves away, the pitch becomes lower. This shift in pitch happens because the sound waves are compressed as the ambulance moves toward you and stretched out as it moves away. There may be something in your embodied hearing of this phenomenon that makes the concept "click."

Of course, examples are also useful if you can merely imagine them, such as recalling what it sounded like the last time you heard an ambulance siren in this way. Videos, animated gifs, and the like can also be extremely useful as examples.

**Plain English**

Technical jargon, though precise, can be alienating and confusing. If you can explain the idea in non-technical language, as though to someone who did not possess any technical knowledge, then you can access the concept itself with more clarity and immediacy.

The famous Feynman technique, named after physicist Richard Feynman, is based on the power of simple and clear language. The idea is that "If you can't explain it to a six-year-old, you don't understand it yourself." As a corollary, if we can find a way to effectively explain it to a six-year-old, we will improve our own understanding!

For example: "The Doppler Effect happens when sound or light waves change as the source moves. If the source is coming toward you, the waves squish together, making the sound higher. If it's moving away, the waves stretch out, making the sound lower. It's why a train whistle changes pitch as it speeds past."

**Technical definition**

Once you have fully explored the concept from many different angles, you can formalize it in precise and complete technical language. You may need scientific or technical terms, or mathematical expressions to show certain relationships.

Our example might look like this:

The Doppler Effect describes the change in frequency of a wave relative to an observer. The formula is:

$$f' = f \frac{v + v_o}{v + v_s}$$

You might find it interesting to look up the Wikipedia article on "The Doppler Effect" and notice how the abstract concept is approached and explored from all the dimensions covered by the ADEPT framework. Ideally, you would approach your own learning in this same multidimensional way.

To apply the ADEPT concept to your own reading, treat it as a kind of troubleshooting tool. If you're really having trouble "cracking" a new concept or understanding what it's all about, you can often make a breakthrough by just switching up your perspective a little. Change textbooks, find a YouTube video, or ask a fellow student. Explain your confusion, or the challenge you're having, step by step, to a stuffed toy. Ask yourself, what is the concept *not* like? What does this concept look like in the real world, and what are some examples where it's *not* present? The more cognitive handles you make available to yourself, the greater your chances of deep understanding.

**Summary:**

- To fine-tune our own analytical understanding of the things we're learning about, we need to master pigeonholing.

Our attentional resources are limited, so we need to allot our time wisely.
- One way to structure and organize your reading is to think of it in terms of three levels: on the line (literal), between the lines (inferential), and beyond the lines (application and context). Reading a text on multiple levels requires time, effort, and active engagement.
- The SPE method is a way of grasping the proverbial "grammar" of a non-fiction book, i.e., the structure that reveals its arguments, premises, and basic propositions. We consider the **s**tructure and the **p**ropositions of an argument, and then **e**valuate its validity and soundness.
- We can use the ADEPT method to help us gain understanding when learning challenging or complex new concepts. Use metaphors, illustrations, examples, and clear, simple language to hone in on the concept, and keep referring back to the complete technical definition.

## Chapter Six: Analyze and Synthesize

The word synthesis comes to us from the Latin *suntithenai,* meaning to "place together." The term has its origin in chemistry, where it was used to describe **the act of bringing separate reactants together so that they produced something entirely new**. When we synthesize, we are not just placing one thing next to another thing (like a fruit salad), but blending them together (like a fruit smoothie).

To continue our food analogy, synthesizing the things we learn into entirely new concepts is like baking a cake. The cake contains eggs, flour, milk, and so on, but the concept *cake* is an entirely new one, and when it's baked, it does not resemble any of its constituent ingredients.

In this chapter, we're going to be looking at note taking and study techniques that help us synthesize new ideas from the information we gather from various sources, as well as our pre-existing knowledge. In chapters one through five we collected many different "ingredients"; in this chapter, we will consider what it takes to make a delicious cake out of them.

## **Compile a KWL Chart**

If we want to begin synthesizing the new things we learn with the old things we have already learned, it follows that we need to be clear on which is which–and that's not as easy as it may first seem! The KWL method is something that seems rather simplistic and obvious until you apply it and realize that "knowing what you know" is not always straightforward.

A KWL chart is a simple visualization to help you analyze and synthesize information during your learning process and keep track of your progress. It stands for:

- Know
- Want to know

- Learn

This is a structured and organized way to identify clearly what you know and what you don't. The more we can clarify areas of curiosity as well as current knowledge gaps, the more thorough and precise our learning will be. A KWL chart is also a useful thing to compile alongside an ADEPT analysis, as it can help you monitor what you're actually learning, and how well you're scaffolding that new knowledge onto the old.

This kind of organization and reflection is essential if we hope to master intelligent synthesis. It's a little like making sure we have all the ingredients needed to make a cake *before* we start making it; if we go into the process of synthesis when we have poorly understood our own position, it's like beginning a recipe and having to stop halfway because we thought we had an ingredient, but didn't.

Here is how to compile a KWL chart.

### Step 1: Identify what you already know

Print out a chart, design your own, or draw one up by hand with pen and paper. You will simply need a table divided into three columns, one each for K, W, and L. As you prepare to read a text, remind yourself of these three categories. Before reading, spend a few moments identifying what you know about the topic, and note everything you're thinking about: Do you have any questions? Any initial responses or curiosities? Any predictions about what you're going to read?

Consider your previous experiences or any background knowledge that relates to the subject. For example, if you're learning about volcanoes, you might already know that they erupt and release lava. Write down these existing ideas in the K section, even if they seem quite basic. Recall the power of schema activation; this step is not a test, but a way to activate prior knowledge, so that you have a framework to build on as you explore new information.

**Step 2: Identify what you want to know**

Next, reflect on what you want to learn from the piece you're about to read, or the topic in general. Identify questions you have or knowledge gaps that have you feeling curious.

You might need to consider broader goals, too, and your overall learning aim.

For instance, when learning about volcanoes, you might want to know "What actually causes a volcano to erupt?" or "How can scientists predict when a volcano will erupt?" Write these questions down in the W section, or simply make a note of the general focus: "eruptions; mechanisms." This will set a clear direction for the learning process you need to follow.

### Step 3: Reflect on what you've learned

Once you've gathered new information and found some answers to your questions, reflect on what you've learned. In the L section, summarize the new insights you've discovered. For example, after studying volcanoes, you might write, "Volcanoes erupt due to pressure from gases and magma beneath the Earth's surface." But you're not done yet; you need to pause and reflect on these answers.

To properly synthesize what you've learned, you have to see how it connects to your prior knowledge. Is there still something you need to know? What allowed you to find the answer, and how does the question look to you now that you have this understanding? Does your answer trigger another question? This kind of reflection reinforces the new information and solidifies your understanding.

Now, a KWL chart can be used in various ways:

- To test yourself and identify missing information you still need to learn, for example in preparation for an exam.
- To plan and organize study sessions, so you can see precisely what progress you've made, and plan your next study session accordingly.
- To shape and guide a research project, so that as you gather new information, you're also ensuring that you understand it properly.

A KWL chart is a way to conduct a kind of **"knowledge and comprehension audit."** As we compile it, we gain greater insight into both our current learning stage, *and* the material we are interested in. We use analysis and synthesis to create a KWL chart, but a KWL chart also improves our ability to further analyze and synthesize what we're learning.

## **The REST Method**

It's important to understand all the things that synthesis is *not*:

- It is not summarizing
- It is not paraphrasing
- It is not analysis
- It is not inference

In fact, all the above are tools we need to use when we synthesize. To make a summary, we shorten a text to its important details; to paraphrase we reword the important details from our source into our own words; to analyze we break a complex topic down into smaller components; and to infer we use our reason to come to a logical conclusion implied in the text. When we synthesize, we do all these things, and more.

To illustrate the difference between merely reading and comprehending a text, and truly synthesizing it, look at the following examples of how someone might process Aesop's fable, "The Lion and the Mouse."

**Note 1:**

A sleeping lion was startled when a timid mouse ran across his nose. As the lion was about to kill her, the mouse pleaded for her life, promising to repay him someday. Amused, the lion let her go. Later, trapped in a hunter's net, the lion roared for help. The mouse recognized his cry and gnawed through the ropes, freeing him. "You laughed at my promise," said the mouse, "but now you see even a mouse can help a lion."

**Note 2:**

My belief that only the strong and powerful can achieve significant acts has been challenged by the story of "The Lion and the Mouse". This story suggests that individuals, regardless of their strength, size, or status, always have the ability to do good and show kindness. Having read plenty of literature where the hero is seemingly blessed with superhuman abilities, and fated from birth to achieve great things, this story suggests the opposite: that kindness alone can be heroic.

The first note is an excellent summary, paraphrase, and analysis of the classic story.

However, only the second note contains any real synthesis, and its quality of comprehension is an order of magnitude greater than that of the first note. If you want to make the leap between note 1 and note 2, one useful approach to utilize is the REST acronym, which stands for:

- Read at least two different sources about your chosen topic, taking notes. Make use of summaries and paraphrasing to identify key details.

- Edit your notes and merge any ideas that are similar. Analyze and organize the key details, looking for underlying structure and argument.

- Synthesize by combining these notes with your pre-existing knowledge on the topic. Start to make connections and inferences.

- Think about new ideas and connect them to your prior knowledge.

Throughout this process, note taking is essential, and helps you keep track of what you're doing, whether you're synthesizing information in an academic context or merely pursuing personal development. Let's follow the process step by step:

## Step 1: Read and take notes from at least two different sources

Begin by reading two distinct sources on a topic. As you read, take notes on the key points and ideas presented in each source. For example, if studying the benefits of outdoor play, you might read one article about its physical health advantages and another about its mental health benefits. Record the main ideas from each source, focusing on what is most important or relevant.

## Step 2: Edit your notes and combine and condense similar topics

After reading and recording the key points, go through your notes and identify concepts that overlap or are closely related. For instance, both articles might highlight that outdoor play reduces stress and increases happiness. You have identified a third possible variable that connects the two articles conceptually–stress reduction. By editing and combining similar concepts in this way, you create a more cohesive understanding of the topic.

**Step 3: Synthesize your notes with what you already know**

This is where the magic starts to happen. Take your notes and merge them with your existing knowledge on the topic. Remember that you're not just summarizing the information or putting new beside old - you're *integrating* the new knowledge with your existing background knowledge, forming new insights.

For example, you might combine your notes on outdoor play with your prior understanding of the importance of social interaction in child development to create a broader perspective on how outdoor activities can enhance well-being. Or perhaps you have read anthropological texts about the concept of play in different cultures across history, and start to see those older concepts in a whole new light.

These concepts themselves have been previously synthesized with others, and recall to your mind other connected ideas, for example, the change in the way children have been parented over the centuries, the invention of indoor schools, the end of agrarian lifestyles, the rise in mental illness in children, etc.

## Step 4: Think about your new ideas and the bigger picture connections

Reflect. How do these new insights change or enhance your existing understanding of the topic? Often, new ideas and information enter our awareness, but they are somewhat provisional until we can find within our own minds a place for them in our existing network of ideas.

This final step, then, is what allows us to solidify the synthesis we've made. By doing this, we also create an additional node or point of connection in our personal web of knowledge, which can be built on with subsequent learning. With synthesis, we are never just gathering up data and storing knowledge; we are building real understanding of the world and, if we're diligent, something approaching real wisdom.

### How to Filter What You Consume

Particularly if we are self-learning and not following a prescribed academic course, we may easily find ourselves in information overload. We may set out with noble intentions for our personal or professional development with a sincere desire to grow in knowledge and insight. It's so easy, however, to become swamped with information, overwhelmed with the sheer amount of knowledge available. This can lead to exhaustion, distraction, loss of focus, wasted time, and a vague panic that we are somehow never doing enough.

It is not humanly possible to comprehend every piece of information out there, and what's more, the information available varies enormously in quality. Some of what we encounter is not merely worthless, but actively harmful. Such a state of affairs means we need to be adept at filtering. Being able to reliably filter the content we consume will ensure that we don't waste time trying to process and comprehend all the wrong things.

Even if all the material we encountered in our lives is useful somehow, not all of it will be *equally* useful, and so, if we hope to be efficient, we need to prioritize and identify what is truly worth our time.

We need to understand the difference between the signal and the noise.

The *signal* is any content that is relevant and actionable. It is content that is high quality.

The *noise* is whatever is irrelevant or cannot be acted upon. It is content that is low quality.

Unfortunately for us, the signal and the noise always appear together in our perception, so it's up to us to get into the habit of filtering out the useful from the not-so-useful.

**Cutting through the noise**

The quality of the information you consume while studying will shape your understanding, critical thinking, and decision-making in the future. Not all content is created equal—some knowledge will remain relevant for years, while other information will quickly lose its value. By applying effective filters, you can focus on long-lasting, meaningful content and avoid wasting time on material that offers little enduring benefit.

Information will often be presented to you as though it's deathly urgent and must be acted on immediately. Other information will be a fleeting meme or gimmick that pretends to be a highly relevant piece of knowledge now and for all time. Get into the habit of not taking such claims seriously! Ask:

- Will this information still be relevant in 10 days?
- What about in 1 year?
- 5 years?
- 10 years?

You might find more stable and lasting value in ancient wisdom texts, established scientific consensus, or proven techniques and approaches than you would in TikTok trends, "breaking news" on 24/7 news sites, or LinkedIn posts quickly written to capitalize on the latest buzzword. Likewise, if you're trying to make sense of complex new information, look past opinions, details, conjecture, and current fashions, and try to identify the more lasting principles beneath them.

**The Lindy Effect is a simple rule of thumb that suggests that the longer something has been around, the more likely it is to still be around in future.** When deciding what to study, prioritize those texts and resources that have stood the test of time. There will always be someone trying to sell you something or trying to rebrand old wisdom as something new, but you can save yourself time and effort by focusing only on those things with a proven track record.

You can certainly watch a famous YouTube influencer explain certain scientific concepts if you find their approach relatable, for example, but *prioritize* the canonical scientific papers and texts. Likewise, there may be some value in a cheap self-published guide on how to write for social media, but you stand to gain a lot more by reading a classic like Strunk and White's *The Elements of Style* or even more fundamentally, Aristotle's *Rhetoric*.

A final piece of advice is to remember that even the highest-quality information out there still might not warrant your attention. If, for example, your ultimate goals have nothing to do with mastering the art of good writing, then you are essentially wasting your time by reading content to that end, whether high-quality or not. Many procrastinators among us get trapped precisely because it seems like there is so much amazing information out there, and our limited attention spans are split in a thousand different directions.

First understand exactly what you are trying to learn, understand, or discover. Set that goal. Then, when a new piece of information appears in your field of awareness and you have to decide whether to engage with it or not, ask yourself:

- Is the information likely to be true or accurate?
- Even if it's true or accurate, is the material high-quality? (there may be better resources out there)
- Even if it is high-quality, is it relevant?
- Even if it is relevant, is it relevant to you personally, and your specific goal?
- Even if it is relevant to your specific goal, is it relevant right now?
- Even if it is relevant right now, is the information actionable in any way? Do those actions connect to your goal?

If a piece of information can pass all through these questions, it likely deserves your full attention! If it doesn't, you can safely ignore it or set it aside for later. Save your attention for where it's really needed.

## Becoming a Syntopical Reader

"Syntopical" contains the same prefix "syn-" that we find in the word "synthesis." This prefix simply means "with" or "together." **When we are engaging in syntopical reading, we read multiple texts on the same topic, comparing the information in them..**

Again, this is not merely reading one book and then reading another; it is truly reading them *together*, as though there were part of the same larger text. Analytical and critical readings are typically confined to a single text, but we can go further. Syntopical reading means ongoing analysis of everything you read in context with everything else you read, continually comparing and contrasting and analyzing the themes and arguments from multiple works at once.

Syntopical analysis is more or less the skill that the Zettelkasten method aims to develop. Also called "comparative reading," it is the widest reaching, most complex, and most demanding form of learning we can undertake–but it's also the most rewarding.

As we have moved through the chapters of our book, we have explored note taking methods that demand increasingly more from us and our critical and analytical thinking. The type and quality of notes we take reflects the type and quality of our reading:

- **Elementary** reading is reading for comprehension of key facts
- **Inspectional** reading is reading for comprehension of narrative, logical structure, and order
- **Analytical** reading is reading for implicit meaning and interpretation
- **Syntopical** reading is reading of the deepest, broadest kind, where we analyze multiple texts in a broader context

These skills are cumulative; this means that we cannot successfully read in a syntopical way if we haven't first learned to read and comprehend in more foundational ways. Basic reading and comprehension skills are a prerequisite for analytical and critical thinking, and these skills in turn are a pre-requisite for truly syntopical reading.

Naturally gifted readers, thinkers, and autodidacts (people who teach themselves) understand this process and apply themselves to it instinctively. For the rest of us, we need prompting to deliberately steer our reading to its fullest and most mature expression.

Syntopical readers are continually exploring how various authors approach the same subject, comparing their perspectives, and synthesizing their insights into a cohesive understanding. They never stop reading. As a matter of fact, their voracious appetite for learning makes them excellent writers; their ability to synthesis and perspective-switch becomes a source of endless creativity.

Reading syntopically means continuously interrogating new information, asking questions, framing concepts this way and then that way, comparing and contrasting, challenging, condensing, expanding, and so on. It is the most active and most engaged form of reading; it is like a giant conversation that unfolds, but instead of single words or sentences, the dialogue is composed of different texts, concepts, authors, and themes.

When you read (and think) this way, you engage with everything and anything, from scientific articles and philosophical arguments to novels and poetry. You can even broaden your definition of what a text ultimately is, and how to read one, so that intelligently perceiving sound, film, and the natural world itself feels no different from attending a lecture or reading a book. Through syntopical reading, the world around you becomes your partner in discovery, and you weave each new experience into a larger, more insightful narrative–your own.

The Five Steps of Syntopical Reading

**Step 1: Find relevant books, passages, and ideas**

Instead of reading every book cover-to-cover, use inspectional reading to identify which sections of each text address your specific questions. Skim, scan, and filter to assess the usefulness of new information.

Suppose you're interested in exploring the topic of leadership during wartime. Don't bother with books that don't address this topic, even tangentially. However, be selective even with the books that do address your topic. In *The Prince* by Machiavelli, for example, focus only on chapters discussing the qualities of effective rulers. In *Team of Rivals* by Doris Kearns Goodwin, zero in on Lincoln's decision-making during the Civil War. Skim both books for sections on wartime strategies and alliances and skip the rest.

**Step 2: Establish common terms**

Each author may use different terminology or frameworks, so it will probably be necessary to create your own consistent set of terms.

If you're investigating the broad theme of "courage," for example, Aristotle in *Nicomachean Ethics* might discuss it as a virtue lying somewhere between recklessness and cowardice, while Brené Brown in *Daring Greatly* talks about vulnerability as a form of courage. They are very different languages, but they're discussing the same concept.

To reconcile these views, you might need to proactively define "courage" for yourself as the ability to act meaningfully in the face of fear.

This term can accommodate both Aristotle's and Brene Brown's expression, and perhaps point to something more fundamental in them both.

### Step 3: Frame your questions

If you think of syntopical reading as an enormous intertextual conversation, then be aware that you will have to direct this conversation among the authors, and between works. Brene Brown never met Aristotle, so you will have to be the intellectual intermediary for that "conversation" between them.

Just as each author will use different terms and expressions to discuss their concepts, they will also possess their own mental models, frameworks, and sets of interpretive lenses. To understand these, and to understand how to compare and contrast between two very different authors, you need to continually ask questions. For example, if your area of inquiry is "freedom," then your questions might include:

- What is the definition of freedom?
- What are the barriers to freedom?

- What is the opposite of freedom?
- How can freedom be achieved or preserved?
- Where does freedom actually come from?

Rousseau in *The Social Contract* might focus on freedom as collective sovereignty, while John Stuart Mill in *On Liberty* emphasizes individual autonomy. Your questions guide how you extract their insights on their own terms and fit them into your overarching understanding. If you simply read both works using nothing more than *your* conception of freedom, you would have done a disservice to both authors–and missed some key information.

## Step 4: Define the issues

As you compare and contrast the answers to these questions, identify points of agreement, disagreement, or nuance in the authors' arguments.

Returning to the example of "freedom," you might find that Rousseau argues that individual freedom must sometimes yield to collective will, and that Mill counters that personal liberty should only be limited to prevent harm to others. This is an interesting point of possible overlap, and something to further explore.

Hannah Arendt in *The Human Condition* introduces a third perspective, focusing on freedom as the ability to act in public spaces. After you read this work, you are able to start framing the debate between Rousseau and Mill in terms of the balance between personal liberty and societal needs. Grouping these perspectives into a structured dialogue in this way helps you gain a richer appreciation of each author, and the connections between them.

**Step 5: Analyze the discussion**

Finally, synthesize the conversation. What insights have you gained? Having started to answer your own questions, what are the implications of these answers? What new questions do they inspire?

After reading Rousseau and Mill for a time, you start to synthesize your own take on the debate; you agree that individual rights are essential if we value innovation and dissent, but you appreciate Arendt's perspective, and the subtly it adds in suggesting that civic engagement is actually a way to sustain and preserve individual freedom.

Many years later, this entire debate again pops into your mind when you begin to read about Confucian philosophy. It's as though another fascinating guest has entered your imaginary dinner party, and has started sharing new ideas about freedom, about the relationship between the individual and "heaven," and about how personal conduct, social relations, and governance are not separate things, but expressions of a single, unified flow...

The old Rousseau-Mill-Arendt debate is pulled out again, dusted off, and examined once more through a new lens. The analysis and synthesis continues. Happily, as long as there is new information to encounter, the syntopical reader's work is never done.

**Summary:**

- Synthesis is bringing separate things together to produce something entirely new. It requires we build new knowledge on prior knowledge. A KWL chart can help us clearly discern between things we still need to learn, and things we have already learned, as well as track our progress from one to the other.

- The REST method is a higher-order tool for synthesizing information from a wide range of sources. Though synthesis requires the tools of summary, analysis, inference, and paraphrasing, it is not itself any of these things.

- In a world drenched with information, it's important to filter what you consume. Prioritize material that is actionable, relevant, high-quality, and has stood the test of time.

- There are four types of reading, in order of depth of comprehension and active engagement: elementary reading is reading for key facts, inspectional reading is reading for logical structure and order, analytical reading is reading for implicit meaning and interpretation, and syntopical reading is reading of the deepest, broadest kind, entailing analysis of multiple sources.

- Syntopical readers read continuously and widely, sifting out common themes, comparing and contrasting, carefully framing questions to help them define and refine those common themes, and ultimately produce a meta "conversation" that forms the basis of their own rich learning and understanding.

www.ingramcontent.com/pod-product-compliance
Lightning Source LLC
Chambersburg PA
CBHW060603080526
44585CB00013B/674